GW00385078

Penguin Monarchs

THE HOUSES OF WESSEX AND DENMARK

THE HOUSES OF NORMANDY, BLOIS AND ANJOU

THE HOUSE OF PLANTAGENET

THE HOUSES OF LANCASTER AND YORK

THE HOUSE OF TUDOR

Henry VII	Sean Cunningham
Henry VIII	John Guy
Edward VI	Stephen Alford
Mary I	John Edwards
Elizabeth I	Helen Castor

THE HOUSE OF STUART

James I	Thomas Cogswell
Charles I	Mark Kishlansky
[Cromwell	David Horspool]
Charles II	Clare Jackson
James II	David Womersley
William III & Mary II	Jonathan Keates
Anne	Richard Hewlings

THE HOUSE OF HANOVER

George I	Tim Blanning
George II	Norman Davies
George III	Amanda Foreman
George IV	Stella Tillyard
William IV	Roger Knight
Victoria	Jane Ridley

THE HOUSES OF SAXE-COBURG & GOTHA AND WINDSOR

Edward VII	Richard Davenport-Hines
George V	David Cannadine
Edward VIII	Piers Brendon
George VI	Philip Ziegler
Elizabeth II	Douglas Hurd

MARK KISHLANSKY

Charles I

An Abbreviated Life

ALLEN LANE

an imprint of

PENGUIN BOOKS

ALLEN LANE

Published by the Penguin Group
Penguin Books Ltd, 80 Strand, London WC2R ORL, England
Penguin Group (USA) Inc., 375 Hudson Street, New York, New York 10014, USA
Penguin Group (Canada), 90 Eglinton Avenue East, Suite 700, Toronto, Ontario,
Canada M4P 2Y3 (a division of Pearson Penguin Canada Inc.)
Penguin Ireland, 25 St Stephen's Green, Dublin 2, Ireland (a division of Penguin Books Ltd)
Penguin Group (Australia), 707 Collins Street, Melbourne, Victoria 3008, Australia
(a division of Pearson Australia Group Pty Ltd)
Penguin Books India Pvt Ltd, 11 Community Centre, Panchsheel Park,
New Delhi – 110 017, India
Penguin Group (NZ), 67 Apollo Drive, Rosedale, Auckland 0632, New Zealand
(a division of Pearson New Zealand Ltd)
Penguin Books (South Africa) (Pty) Ltd, Block D, Rosebank Office Park,
181 Jan Smuts Avenue, Parktown North, Gauteng 2193, South Africa

Penguin Books Ltd, Registered Offices: 80 Strand, London WC2R ORL, England

www.penguin.com

First published 2014
001

Set in 9.5/13.5 pt Sabon LT Std
Typeset by Jouve (UK), Milton Keynes
Printed in Great Britain by Clays Ltd, St Ives plc

ISBN: 978-0-141-97983-0

www.greenpenguin.co.uk

Contents

For the three Ms

Preface

I have lived with Charles I for more years than I care to remember. With such intimacy comes ambivalence. He was a man and a monarch who has never been given his due even if his reign was a disaster for his three kingdoms. Highlighting his virtues downplays his faults, while emphasizing his vices downplays his achievements. Removing some blame from Charles's shoulders and placing it on those of his opponents rebalances our understanding of the mid-seventeenth-century crisis. Such an undertaking is not likely to make Charles or this author more popular. But a shift of perspective opens wide new vistas of historical understanding. It is hoped that seeing the king from his point of view will force a re-evaluation of historical interpretations that have remained unchanged for centuries.

It was Montaigne who first said, 'I wrote you a long letter because I didn't have time to write a short one.' Writing an abbreviated biography was an equally terrifying challenge. It enforced not only an economy of style, but an economy of perspective. Relating only what the reader needed to know in order to follow the story meant ignoring much of significance and making hard choices. In all cases I have opted for narrative flow rather than interpretive complexity. My aim has been to make Charles an easy read despite his being a complex man.

During the time frame of this study, England used the Julian calendar in which the year was reckoned to begin on 25 March. In this book, all dates are given New Style with the year beginning on 1 January. In an aristocratic society, men acquired titles and elevations of rank during their lifetime. I have taken the liberty of designating them by the title by which they are known historically even if they hadn't yet received it by strict chronology. Finally, matters of money present challenges both historical and contemporaneous. Most statements of royal revenue and debt are approximations and are best used as comparisons rather than absolutes. For the curious, there are a number of calculators of the historical worth of money. In spending value, £100 in 1625 is equivalent to £16,000 in today's money. Finally, spelling and punctuation have been modernized in quotations from primary sources.

Mark Kishlansky
Cambridge, Mass.

Prologue

'Even his virtues were misinterpreted and scandalously reviled. His gentleness was miscalled defect of wisdom; his firmness, obstinacy; his regular devotion, popery; his decent worship, superstition; his opposing of schism, hatred of the power of godliness.'[1]

Charles I is the most despised monarch in Britain's historical memory. Considering that among his predecessors were murderers, rapists, psychotics and the mentally challenged, this is no small distinction. In most modern accounts, he is portrayed as a mean, petty and vindictive tyrant who brought misery to his subjects and ruin to his nation. However, Charles did not earn these censures by having an aberrant personality; indeed his characteristics were mostly laudable. He had refined sensibilities and loved art, music and dance as a connoisseur rather than as a dilettante. He was a religious man, at prayers daily, attentive to sermons, and he died a martyr to his Church. Abstemious, he dined moderately and diluted his wine to keep a clear head. His court was in decorous contrast to the boisterous one he inherited. 'He himself was never obscene in his speech, or affected it in others.'[2] Moreover, Charles was an uxorious husband, the only seventeenth-century monarch who took neither mistresses nor lovers, and a doting father before his children were ripped from him by the disaster of civil war. He even aspired to make England a great European power. All of this should have weighed in his favour.

Charles lived in an age that attributed historical catastrophes to the will and personality of individuals. In a monarchy, the king was the obvious prime mover. But many contemporaries found only modest faults in his character. The Earl of Clarendon, who knew the king better than most, believed that he was too soft, unwilling to slip the iron fist inside the velvet glove. The Archbishop of Canterbury's chaplain, Peter Heylyn, who also observed the king first hand, remembered 'a maxim of King Charles that it was better to be deceived, than to distrust'. This piety, Heylyn regretted, 'proved a plain and easy way unto those calamities which afterwards were brought upon him'.[3] The king's inclination to bestow benefit of the doubt made him slow to react to challenges to his authority, which led inevitably to greater challenges. For this reason Sir Philip Warwick, who attended the king in his last years, characterized him as 'a gracious and a serious prince, by diversity of counsels drawn off from his own judgment'.[4] If these were grievous faults, then grievously did he pay for them.

The process of demonization began in the 1640s among Parliamentarians who blackened the reputation of the king. They spoke of tyranny and claimed that the monarch had pursued 'a malignant and pernicious design of subverting the fundamental laws and principles of government'.[5] Their tactics gained early support but soon rebounded against them. To destroy the Earl of Strafford, Charles's chief minister, they spun a fantasy of a king so bent on destroying his own people that he planned to turn an Irish army loose in England. Thus when it became necessary to raise an army to suppress the Irish Rebellion, it was impossible for Parliament to trust the king to lead it. While overt criticism of Charles in Parliament was still largely muted in the early 1640s, the unlicensed press proved less circumspect. The king was satirized, caricatured and traduced. All of this made it possible to take up arms against him and ultimately to bring him to his death.

The Parliamentarian view of Charles has held sway for generations. What began as propaganda has been transmuted into seeming fact. Psychoanalysis of his personality became irresistible: 'he was the nervous man afraid of seeming nervous, the shy man afraid of seeming shy'.[6] Much is made of the childhood speech defect that he worked diligently to overcome and was absent from his most public oratory, including the speeches he gave during his trial. One historian has pondered whether his stutter 'was a symptom of some deep-seated neurosis, coming possibly from the fear of his father, rejection by his mother, or domination by an elder brother that haunted Charles for most of his life'.[7] According to this interpretation, Charles's supposed haughtiness masked a deep-seated insecurity: 'He had a stubborn and authoritarian temperament, and was both secretive and impatient.'[8] His style of government has often been maligned as inflexible. He would 'brook no compromise [and] believe that his word was final', an odd criticism of a king.[9] Other historians have drawn the opposite conclusion and found Charles too timorous to rule effectively: 'Charles consistently exhibited insecurity, lack of confidence and weakness.'[10] Among modern interpreters a consensus long ago formed around the view 'that Charles I, whatever his virtues, was unfit to be a king'.[11]

In one of the most influential accounts of the twentieth century, G. M. Trevelyan described Charles as 'a stupid and selfish' man.[12] This judgement has been repeated so often that historians inclined towards a more balanced view are reduced to the faintest of praise: Charles was 'not stupid but his mind was narrow and inflexible'.[13] 'An awe-inspiring degree of crass stupidity' is a remarkable description of one of the most cultured and cultivated monarchs to have occupied the English throne.[14] Charles's principled stands have come to be interpreted as 'a rigid inability to compromise' matched with a 'transparent dishonesty'.[15] This has been the dominant assessment in recent decades.

Peeling away these layers of hostile interpretation is no easy task. Some allegations can be easily refuted, such as the baseless charge that he was 'totally humourless'.[16] In fact, Charles revealed his ready wit on many occasions. When he demanded that a parliamentary officer sent to apprehend him produce instructions authorizing the outrage, the cornet pointed to his arrayed troops, prompting from Charles the mordant concession that 'his instructions were in fair characters and legible without spelling'.[17] He once admonished Strafford with the wry advice 'I will end with a rule that may serve for a statesman, a courtier, or a lover – never make a defence or apology before you be accused.'[18] He also had a playful side. He made a wager with Lord Falkland, one of his courtiers, claiming that he could identify anything written by Sir Edward Hyde, who frequently drafted documents in the king's name. One day, Falkland brought Charles a bundle of tracts printed in London, one of which was an anonymous piece of propaganda penned by Hyde but attributed to two Parliamentarians. When the king failed to recognize the true author, Falkland demanded his winnings, 'which his majesty in the instant apprehending, blushed, and put his hand in his pocket, and gave him an angel, saying, he had never paid a wager more willingly; and was very merry upon it'.[19]

Other charges – for example, the claim that he was perfidious – are more persistent. According to one recent account, 'negotiating with Charles must often have felt like dealing with someone whose fingers were permanently crossed behind his back'.[20] This assumption that he would repudiate his word is indeed baseless speculation quite incompatible with what we know of his private thoughts. From the beginning of the war, Queen Henrietta Maria pleaded with her husband to promise whatever was demanded of him so that he could resume power. From her point of view, Charles was negotiating with heretics and with a gun to his head. Concessions born of necessity carried no moral obligation. Charles never saw it that way. He consistently attempted to stand on his principles and find compromises that he could bear. In this effort he was consistently rebuffed. There is certainly no evidence that Charles was 'perfidious, not only from constitution and from habit, but also on principle'.[21]

In his relations with foreign rulers, he kept the promises that served English interests and ignored the ones that did not. Such were the ways of statecraft in the lawless global state of nature, and it is truly said that he 'was not more deceitful than most rulers'.[22] There is certainly no reason to portray his failures to live up to the terms of his French marriage treaty or his Spanish alliance as character defects. Once the civil wars broke out, he was frequently placed in untenable situations in which he made incompatible offers to competing factions. However, offers are not promises and a close examination of the record shows that he almost never made promises that he did not keep.

Just as the king's reputation for deceit and double-dealing is wildly overblown, so too is his alleged failure to compromise. Indeed, it is hard to find an instance of such behaviour in his dealings with his early parliaments, with the Scots or in the manifold peace negotiations during the civil wars. Compromise was often Charles's first instinct. In the most famous instance of his supposed obduracy, when he imprisoned those who rioted in the House of Commons in 1629, it is often overlooked that the king offered to release any MP who would recognize his fault. Sir John Eliot, one of the king's most vocal opponents, stood stiff and died in captivity; Denzil Holles, though equally hostile to Charles, pledged good behaviour and was released. Similarly, Charles welcomed into his government many who had opposed him in Parliament. The Earl of Strafford, a parliamentary critic of royal government in 1628, was only the most prominent of the so-called patriots who came to serve the king. By 1640 he was his primary adviser.

Charles's reputation as authoritarian and uncompromising has led historians to blame him for the failure of the peace negotiations that punctuated the civil wars. This is surprising in that it was the king alone who made concessions to Parliament's non-negotiable demands. He frequently demeaned the parliamentary commissioners as letter carriers when they informed him that they had no power to treat. Where he was willing to find compromise solutions, first the Scots and then the Parliamentarians remained obdurate.

The fact that Charles I is misunderstood does not mean, of course, that he is a sympathetic figure, still less a successful one. He failed decisively in the chief obligation laid on a monarch, to bequeath his kingdoms to his heir. His reign was marred by the kind of religious unrest unknown since the reign of Queen Mary as well as by unprecedented political agitation. Once the exogenous crisis of the Scottish rebellion occurred, politics and religion combined into the conflagration of civil war. His rule triggered deep emotional responses in many of his subjects, leading them to risk life and fortune to oppose him. We cannot know whether the concessions he made in 1641–2, and the ones he was willing to make in 1648, would have been sufficient to knit the nation back together.

'For my part I do believe he was not the worst, but the most unfortunate of kings,' the astrologer William Lilly reflected.[23] The catalogue of near misses is long. The Spanish fleet carrying South American treasure against which Charles sent a flotilla in 1625 narrowly evaded capture; the expedition led by the Duke of Buckingham, Charles's admiral, chief minister and best friend, against the Ile de Ré in 1628 would have succeeded except for a freak shift of the winds; the Battle of Naseby could easily have turned in the king's favour. Had the outcomes of any of these events been different, Charles's reign would have run another course entirely. 'Wisdom and Reason were not wanting in that Noble King; Fortune was.'[24] This is not to say that the king bore no responsibility for his military failures. His eagerness to show his intentions in 1625 led to launching an inadequate fleet too late in the campaign season to achieve its objectives. His decision to send Buckingham to Ile de Ré without the reinforcement and resupply necessary to sustain the siege meant that, once the wind shifted, Buckingham had no choice but to retreat through a lethal crossfire. He overruled the superior judgement of his general and nephew, Prince Rupert, that Naseby was not the place to make a winner-take-all stand.

Beneath the reviled and excoriated king of historical reputation is a flesh-and-blood man trapped by circumstances he could not control and events he could not shape. He had personal shortcomings and he made some glaring errors. But it is time for his reputation to be re-examined, his aspirations recognized and his accomplishments acknowledged. Such an investigation will provide insights not only into the nature of seventeenth-century monarchy, but also into the causes and development of the civil wars in Charles's kingdoms. The legacy of Charles I should no longer be measured by his faults alone.

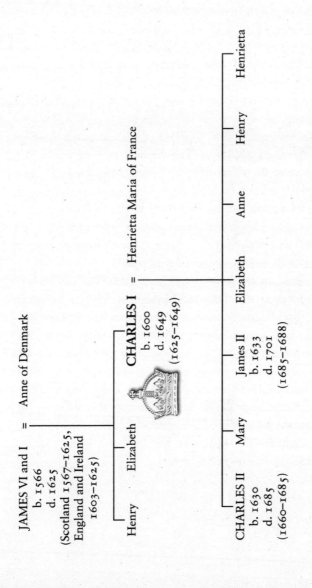

Charles I

I
Prince and King

Charles I remains the only monarch in Britain's history to be tried, condemned and publicly executed. This extraordinary end had an ordinary beginning. He was born in Scotland in 1600, second son of James VI and his Danish wife, Anne. In 1603 these Scottish royals inherited from the childless Queen Elizabeth the throne of England and suzerainty over Ireland. England in the seventeenth century was still a minor European power. It had a population of less than four million, 10 per cent living in its capital, London. In what was predominantly an agricultural nation, the vast majority of people farmed for their subsistence. England was also highly stratified, with perhaps 2 per cent of the people owning 98 per cent of the wealth. Large estates were kept intact through primogeniture, which privileged the interests of eldest sons. The small titular nobility and larger gentry prized lineage above all. Both had benefited by the Reformation and the break-up and sale of the monastic lands of the outlawed Catholic Church, while among the gentry many families solidified their fortunes though profits from trade and the law.

Though London was a thriving port that trafficked in the goods of the world, England's exports were limited to unfinished cloth that was mainly marketed to the Low Countries. Exploration brought colonies in North America and the Caribbean, but these remained fledgling settlements that needed nourishment. Safe in its island fastness, England had no standing army, little artillery and decaying fortifications. However, it was a sea power of the first rank, albeit one dependent on the capacity to arm its merchant fleet in times of necessity. Its reputation was won by the defeat of the Spanish Armada in 1588, an occasion when the fortune of the winds turned in England's favour.

The accession of James I joined Scotland and England under a single monarch, but it was a regal rather than an incorporative union. The two nations maintained separate governing bodies, distinctive Churches and their own legal systems. All they shared was a monarch, a Scotsman who now resided in Westminster.

The nation may have been comparatively poor in material resources but it was rich in artistic achievement. The England inherited by James I was experiencing a literary renaissance without parallel, its writers creating works that would live for centuries. New plays by Shakespeare were an annual event in the century's first decade and they competed with the equally popular productions of Ben Jonson. John Donne's poetry circulated in manuscript, while the great works of Philip Sidney, Edmund Spenser and Francis Bacon were immortalized in print. Entertainment at court was enlivened with the introduction of masques, Italianate pageants of music, dance and theatre often performed by courtiers (and occasionally by the queen herself). Inigo Jones, who designed Covent Garden and the royal Banqueting House, was enlisted to create dramatic special effects, including fireworks, engines that lifted performers into artificial clouds, and noise machines that imitated thunder and storms. Transcending all, the most beloved work in the English language, the King James Bible, was published in 1611.

It was into this world that Charles Stuart was born. Owing to his physical infirmities, he was obliged to remain in Scotland when his family removed south. There he was under the care of Lord Fyvie, later Earl of Dunfermline, who, because of the child's ill-health, despaired for his survival. The young prince was born with a speech defect that caused him to stutter and, like his father, rickets that weakened his ankles. A special boot with brass inserts was manufactured to help him stand until his bones strengthened. By dint of hard work, he overcame both these obstacles, becoming a successful tournament competitor and a more than capable debater. In later life it was observed, 'when he walked on foot, he rather trotted than paced, he went so fast'.[1] There is no truth to assertions that his parents shunned him. While Charles remained in Scotland, reports of his development were regularly despatched to James. When, in 1604, he was well enough to travel under the supervision of his new guardian, Sir Robert Carey, the king and queen rode into Northamptonshire to meet him, 'very glad to see their young son'.[2]

Charles had a conventional princely education, one part humanist curriculum and one part vigorous physical exertion. He loved reading and developed a life-long passion for the plays of Shakespeare. The moderate Scottish Presbyterian and subsequent Provost of Eton Thomas Murray oversaw his training and fed him a steady diet of classics and Protestant theology. To apprise his father of his progress in languages, Charles sent letters in Latin and French, which was in compliance with James's method of monitoring his children's upbringing. 'I have been bred up at Gamaliel's feet,' Charles was proud to say, in reference to the great Hebrew teacher.[3] The prince was accounted 'a good mathematician, not unskilful in music, well read in divinity, excellently in history, and no less in the laws and statutes of this nation'.[4]

Charles's youth was occupied in preparation for the responsibilities he would inherit. Even as a child he exhibited the determination that his critics would later call stubbornness. He was described by one of his early chaplains as 'sober, grave, [and] sweet'.[5] He received the usual honours due his high station, being made Duke of York and Knight of the Bath in 1605 and Knight of the Garter in 1611. At the age of nine, he adopted as a motto 'if you would conquer all things, submit yourself to reason'.[6] Charles was close to his elder brother, the crown prince Henry, who responded to his childish earnestness by threatening to make him an archbishop. He was closer still to his sister, Elizabeth. One of Charles's earliest letters was written to offer his brother possession of his favourite toys. At ten years, no longer lame, he danced at Henry's installation as Prince of Wales where he had the honour of presenting Henry with the ceremonial sword. Charles adored his mother and venerated his father. She returned his love, bequeathing him her personal estate. But he always had to compete for James's affection, first with his brother and then with a succession of his father's male lovers. These trials did not harden him; indeed there was no slander that more deeply shocked him than the recurring allegation that he had poisoned his father.

This privileged life of reading, riding and revelry with his siblings came to an abrupt end in 1613. As Charles was overseeing preparation of a masque to celebrate Elizabeth's impending nuptials to Frederick, Elector Palatine, word came that his brother had been taken ill. Charles arrived at his bedside to find him beset by an elevated fever and depressed physicians. He played cards with the prince during his final days and was present to the end. At the age of twelve, it fell to him to act as chief mourner in his brother's funeral, a role he would reprise when his mother died in 1619. On both occasions, his father took to his bed and left his son to perform the obsequies.

Charles's life changed profoundly after Prince Henry died. He inherited a palace, a court and a retinue but not the adulation showered on his brother by those who hoped for a future Protestant renaissance. This dream died with James's vivacious firstborn and Charles lacked the charisma to reawaken it. Though he had the same upbringing, the same religious training and the same outlook, his temperament was different. He was less open and outgoing than was his brother and he could never inspire the same loyalty. Throughout his teenage years, he found himself chasing evasive expectations. At the same time, he lost his sister, his other childhood companion. In the weeks after Henry's passing, the siblings had consoled each other; but within months, Elizabeth sealed her marriage to the elector and took ship to the Palatinate. Charles would never see her again.

Now heir to the throne, the young duke found his life became more regimented. James had him carefully groomed in order to hasten his preparation for kingship. Inheriting the title Duke of Cornwall, he had his own revenue and consequently a larger retinue. He acquired his brother's Calvinist chaplains, fierce anti-Catholic polemicists, who stepped up his religious education. In 1613 he made his confirmation under the strict examination of James Montague, Calvinist Bishop of Winchester.

In the following year, Charles rode to the opening of Parliament and accompanied his father on summer progress and hunts. He visited both Oxford and Cambridge Universities, the former awarding him a degree in 1616. Interested in military affairs, the prince reviewed the trained bands of the London militia. As a boy he had enjoyed deploying artillery and armies of toy soldiers to recreate historical battles. Once his sister departed, he made himself expert in the affairs of the Holy Roman Empire and conversed with foreign diplomats about the state of European politics. At his sixteenth birthday, he was installed as Prince of Wales in the same elaborate ceremony that had elevated his brother. A golden ring was placed on his finger and a golden rod in his hand, symbolic of the revenue that derived from the Welsh principality, income that again expanded his court. Also in this year came the English publication of King James's collected works, dedicated to Charles with the motto 'I have given thee a wise and understanding heart'.[7]

Among them, *Basilikon Doron*, or 'king's gift', was a guide-book for a prince destined for the crown.

Charles's personal isolation did not last long. In 1615 his father showered his affections on a new favourite, George Villiers, subsequently Duke of Buckingham. Villiers proved to be a perfect companion for the young prince. Eight years his senior, Villiers was worldly wise. He had spent three years on the continent acquiring the patina of gallantry that added to his exceptional good looks and courtly manners. After a few missteps, the two quickly became friends and companions. Villiers was knighted with Charles's sword and the prince, who was titularly Lord Admiral, surrendered the office to him as a gift. They shared a taste in horses, military matters and especially Italian art. They sat together on the naval commission in which Charles developed his lifelong commitment to English sea power. But where Charles was sexually innocent, Villiers was more than guilty. He shared a bed with the ageing king, who favoured him above all others and nicknamed him Steenie, an affectionate appellation that the prince also adopted. Villiers, following the king, called him Baby Charles, but by 1616 observers as astute as Francis Bacon had concluded 'the prince grows up fast to be a man'.[8]

This was seen in 1619, the year of illnesses. First his mother became sick and declined rapidly. Again it was Charles who conducted the deathbed vigil and who appeared as chief mourner at a dismal event. Court watchers praised his dignified demeanour, 'with an auspicious and a dropping eye', and believed it constituted his coming of age.[9] Shortly afterwards, the king contracted an illness and retired to Royston with his full complement of doctors. Charles was summoned to hear what James believed would be his dying declaration. The old king exhorted him to defend the established Church, to protect his sister and to favour Buckingham. After this traumatic encounter, James recovered. Next it was Buckingham's turn to approach death's door. Now, both king and prince kept vigil for his eventual recovery. James continued to shower his favourite with gifts and privileges. Landless in 1615, Villiers acquired a massive estate five years later, including income from marriage to Katherine Manners, the richest heiress in England. George, Charles and James acted as a powerful triumvirate until events in Germany demonstrated the prince's independent outlook.

Like most of the Protestant rulers of Europe, Frederick, Elector Palatine, was approached by the Calvinist leaders of Bohemia and offered their kingship. This was a poisoned chalice because Ferdinand Habsburg, the Catholic Holy Roman Emperor, believed the crown to be his by historical right. His determination to fight for it had persuaded less ambitious princes to refuse the Bohemian offer, but Frederick dreamed of elevation and his wife Elizabeth encouraged him even if she never actually said that she 'would rather eat sauerkraut with a king than roast meat with an elector'.[10] James was mortified by Frederick's decision and did everything in his power to dissuade his son-in-law. But Charles was ebullient. He stated publicly that he was glad of Frederick's intervention, studied the Bohemian situation and pledged £10,000 of his own revenue to support the new king. Indeed, he volunteered to lead an English military expedition into Germany, but James would not hear of it. When the elector's forces were routed in 1620 at the Battle of White Mountain near Prague, Charles was devastated. His sister now lobbied him for support that he was powerless to provide.

Thus, at the age of twenty, Charles began his practical political education. He supported the calling of the parliament in 1621 and faithfully attended the sessions of the House of Lords. Though not yet an official member of the Privy Council, the highest council in the realm, he was frequently found at its meetings. How much his father shared his plans with him is unknown. At this point Charles was squarely in the camp of those militants who wanted to support the Protestant cause in a religiously divided Europe. But a parliament was never focused on just one issue. While Charles's experience in the Lords was positive, he viewed the actions of the Commons with increasing alarm. The Lower House begrudgingly assented to the king's request for war finance, but it also moved against his ministers, impeaching Lord Chancellor Francis Bacon for corruption. Complaints against monopolies escalated into an attack upon Buckingham. Then, James's diplomatic overtures were openly discussed in violation of the royal prerogative. Worse still, Charles's marriage prospects became a topic of public debate, to the consternation of king and prince. Confrontation between king and Commons led to an early dissolution and the loss of the subsidies that James needed in order to rattle his sabre.

While the king had no desire for military adventures, he had an elaborate plan for the recovery of the Palatinate through a diplomatic marriage. Initially, Elizabeth's marriage to the Protestant elector was to be paired with Henry's to the Catholic Infanta of Spain. Now James revived these plans with Charles as the prospective bridegroom. The scheme was for an Anglo-Spanish union sealed by the return of Frederick's estates that the Spanish and Austrian Habsburgs had overrun. There was reason for James to believe that he could win a diplomatic victory without risking military action. The carrot was the restoration of peace in Central Europe; the stick was potential English intervention in the war. The Spanish were vulnerable to English naval actions against their supply ships or, worse, attacks on their ports. Though Charles had been raised a staunch Calvinist, he was willing to endure the complications of an inter-faith marriage: 'at bottom this concerns my sister'.[11] Negotiations began in earnest in 1620 but proceeded laboriously. The refusal of the parliament of 1621 to stoke anti-Catholic war fever weakened James's bargaining position, though progress was slowly won. For their part, the Spanish needed to keep England neutral while their armies continued to sweep through the Palatinate.

In 1623 Charles decided to take the bit between his own teeth. Believing the enthusiastic reports of James's ambassador, the Earl of Bristol, the prince persuaded his father to allow him to conclude the negotiations personally. His argument that James himself had travelled to Denmark to woo his wife was supported by Buckingham, who volunteered to chaperone Charles. The two of them set out together on what they called the 'voyage of the knights of adventure' and travelled incognito through France. They reached Madrid at the beginning of Easter week, to the consternation of the English embassy and the confusion of the Spanish government. Philip IV and his principal adviser, the conde-duque de Olivares, mistakenly concluded that Charles intended to convert to Catholicism.

After conferring with Bristol, Buckingham took the lead in negotiating and was soon bogged down in the details of the religious settlement that had to be hammered out not only with the leaders of the Spanish Church, but also with the pope. Meanwhile, Charles was given a reception worthy of a prince. The Spanish staged a mock battle for his entertainment and he dined in elaborate court style. The formality of the Spanish court made an abiding impression on him, as did the austere manners of his eighteen-year-old host. Charles toured Madrid, purchased art, including two Titians, and had his portrait painted by Velasquez. In accordance with the complex rules of courtship, he was only allowed glimpses of the infanta, first as she rode in a carriage through a park and then as she sat in a garden. Ultimately, he was allowed to present the rich presents he had brought including 'a rope of pearls and an anchor of great diamonds'.[12] He professed himself smitten.

The adventurers wrote to James daily, but week after week they reported little of substance. As soon as the religious issues were seemingly resolved, Pope Gregory XV died and everything had to begin again. More worryingly, the marriage contract was proceeding without any mention of the Palatinate. Olivares proposed that the restored lands be given to the couple as a wedding gift, an unenforceable offer. James and Charles believed that this had to be the quid pro quo for allowing the infanta to raise her children in her own faith and for abandoning the persecution of English Catholics. When news of these concessions was made public, they would be deeply unpopular; indeed, the marriage itself was excoriated in illegally printed tracts and manuscript libels that circulated widely in England. James gambled that if the threat to European Protestantism was eliminated, so would be the unpopularity of the marriage. Yet little progress was being made in this direction. Charles began to feel himself a prisoner in Spain, albeit one in a golden cage, and he made the tactical decision to conclude the marriage terms and return home. He came to realize that the Spanish Habsburgs would never relinquish their control of Frederick's lands or use their influence with their Austrian cousins. His private correspondence revealed that his initial optimism had given way to deep distrust of both the Spanish negotiators and his father's ambassador. Having arrived with a heart brimming with love for his intended bride, he left with one filled with hate for her father's government.

The return of the bachelor-prince to England was met with celebration. Crowds cheered him as he made his way to Westminster and bonfires illuminated London. There was genuine relief for his safety but also exhilaration over the failure of the much-detested Spanish match. Charles and Buckingham bombarded James with tales of Spanish perfidy: of their efforts to convert the prince to Catholicism, their refusal to discuss the Palatinate, and of their obvious stalling tactics. Diplomacy had failed and they badgered the king to prepare for war. Never before had Charles opposed his father's will; he now demonstrated an unexpected independence that had resulted from his Spanish journey. But war was no easy sell. James's lifelong pacifism was fortified by the incontestable fact that a Spanish marriage was the best hope for Frederick's restoration.

Against this background, Charles and Buckingham urged the calling of Parliament. Though the last two parliaments had ended chaotically, prince and duke promised the king that they could manage a new one. Charles held meetings with potential leaders of the Commons, where he stoked anti-Spanish bellicosity with tales of his humiliation in Madrid. He promised that these 'patriot leaders' would share in the spoils of victory and would receive offices in a Caroline monarchy. Thus the parliament of 1624 opened in a spirit of co-operation. The king asked for advice about his diplomatic commitments and both Houses advised him to break off the treaties with Spain. Three subsidies were voted for military operations, with three more promised in the autumn. Charles personally concluded negotiations for a coalition with the Dutch, while ambassadors to France were hammering out a marriage between Charles and Louis XIII's sister, Henrietta Maria. Nevertheless, not all was smooth sailing. The greatest obstacle was James himself. As the reality of a war closed in, he did everything possible to forestall it. Parliamentary supply was used to hire the soldier of fortune Ernst von Mansfeld and a regiment of mercenaries. Yet when Mansfeld was ready to launch his expedition in January 1625, the king forbade him from entering the Palatinate or engaging with Spanish troops. Instead his forces languished in the Netherlands, consuming money and being consumed by disease. Nor could the king be persuaded to reverse course. James was now visibly deteriorating, physically weak and mentally unstable. At the end of a harsh winter, he took to his bed with shivering fits and a high fever. There he died on 27 March 1625.

2

Wars and Parliaments

Charles was grief-stricken upon the news of his father's death. He had loved James deeply and believed that love had been reciprocated: 'From my infancy I was blessed with the King, my father's love.'[1] Against all precedent, he acted as chief mourner at the grotesquely expensive funeral he personally orchestrated. Sixteen miles of black cloth was distributed for mourning dress and Charles himself was adorned as a penitent rather than a monarch. A decade later he commissioned Rubens to immortalize James in the ceiling panels of the Banqueting House. Throughout his reign he publicly praised James's wisdom and achievements and invoked his memory to authorize his own political, diplomatic and religious policies. Charles and Buckingham consoled each other as both felt the loss keenly.

Nevertheless, the principle that 'the king is dead, long live the king' meant that Charles could not wallow in his grief. Royal decorators replaced 'JR' with 'CR' on thousands of doors, tapestries and arches, while the Royal Mint began stamping the new king's image on coins. Immediately, Charles declared his intention 'to continue all the late King's officers [and] councillors in their charges' and they were all sworn in.[2] He also summoned Lord Keeper John

Williams to St James's Palace and told him a parliament was necessary 'for maintaining the war with Spain'. When Williams informed him that the parliament of 1624 was terminated on his father's death, Charles insisted, over Williams's objections, that writs for a new one be issued without delay: 'the fleet must go forth in the summer'.[3] At the beginning of April, Charles appointed a council of war and began preparations for launching an expedition for England's entrance into the Thirty Years War, the bloodiest conflict yet in Europe's history.

The imminence of Charles's marriage added to the tangle of emotions raised by his father's death. Indeed, in the very week that the king had expired, Buckingham had been scheduled to travel to France to act as proxy in the ceremony. He had prepared a magnificent wardrobe, including a purple satin suit embroidered with pearls said to have cost £20,000. The trip was cancelled and the duc de Chevreuse, dressed in black mourning clothes, acted instead as Charles's stand-in to wed the sixteen-year-old Henrietta Maria, who was described as 'being for her age somewhat little' and 'on the very skirts of womanhood'.[4] The marriage had been necessitated by the failure of the Spanish match. Only France could now provide a dowry sufficient to pay down James's debts and contribute to a naval enterprise. Since Charles's marriage to a French Catholic princess was nearly as unpopular as his engagement to a Spanish one, negotiations had been conducted during the prorogation of the parliament of 1624 to forestall any criticism by MPs.

He had planned to welcome Henrietta Maria at Dover, escort her to London and then open Parliament. But nature intervened. Contrary winds trapped the English convoy in the French Channel ports while Charles idled in Kent. Parliament was postponed first for one week and then for another. Finally the queen made a storm-tossed journey across the Channel to meet her husband for the first time. She was sick from her maiden sea voyage when Charles arrived to claim his marital rights. Henrietta Maria endured her wedding night as an unwelcomed obligation, for the next morning her servants found her morose and the king 'very jocund'.[5] Fireworks and celebrations marked their entry, though in a downpour, to Westminster. Thousands of boats followed them under London Bridge and the banks of the Thames were lined with cheering crowds, all toasting the royal couple.

But behind the pomp was grim circumstance. For, simultaneous with the queen's arrival, London experienced an outbreak of the plague. Within weeks, hundreds were dead and then thousands. The son of one of the king's bakers contracted the disease, causing the royal ovens to be shut down and forcing the king to decamp to Hampton Court. However, Charles remained intent on obtaining war financing from his newly selected parliament. King and queen processed into London on 16 June and Parliament was opened two days later.

The parliament of 1625 assembled in a sour mood. Some members genuinely feared for their lives; others were upset that the monies voted for a war with Spain in 1624 had been wasted on Mansfeld's fruitless expedition. But some particularly influential members felt betrayed that Charles's promise of preferment – 'when time doth serve, you shall find your loves and your labours well bestowed' – was broken by his confirmation of James's officeholders.[6] Acknowledging the anxiety caused by the plague, Charles proposed that the members vote military supply and then adjourn until the autumn when other matters could be considered at leisure. The king did not ask Parliament for a specific sum to launch his war, for two reasons. First, it was customary for Parliament to make a free gift to a new monarch to cover his considerable inaugural expenses. The king could hardly suggest the size of this gift nor did he want it to be conflated with the separate war funding. The second reason was practical. The council of war computed that it needed more than £800,000, a sum impossible to be raised by subsidies. Therefore the king asked the Commons to suggest other forms of military support, a strong signal that he was willing to consider financial reform.

Charles also needed financial support from France and this created a contradiction between his personal Anglicanism and the concessions James had promised regarding English Catholics. In contravention of the marriage treaty, Charles had prohibited his English subjects from attending Mass in the queen's chapel and ostentatiously issued orders that the anti-Catholic laws be enforced. Secretly, he instructed Lord Keeper Williams to delay conveying those orders. Faced with incompatible options, Charles tried to have his cake and eat it. He needed French support for his war and for the payment of the remainder of his wife's dowry, so he had to be seen to be loosening restrictions on Catholics. At the same time, he needed parliamentary subsidies to supply his fleet and thus had to flaunt an honest

English hostility to popery in keeping with the mood of his parliament. Charles did his best to appear faithful to each side. Thus began the myth of his perfidy. It is easy to say that James should not have made the concessions over Catholics in the negotiations, but then there would have been no match, no dowry and no alliance. In hindsight, Charles should have granted Catholic toleration in return for a French subsidy much larger than anything that Parliament would ever provide. But he was a principled Protestant and this solution never tempted him. His single objective was to launch his expedition and each wasted day shortened the period of calm seas and fair winds necessary for its success.

Charles approached his first assembly of his subjects in a spirit of co-operation. He described himself as a 'prince of parliaments'. This was a notion of which his MPs would soon disabuse him. He and Buckingham had successfully moved the previous parliament to give generously and there was no apparent reason why this one should not do the same. They were nonplussed to discover that the 1625 parliament raised every possible objection to their plans. While debating supply, members insisted on being informed about the nature of the war. Some favoured a limited campaign of privateering against Spanish shipping in the West Indies, in the manner of the parsimonious Queen Elizabeth and her Sea Dogs; others accepted the need for a continental invasion to recover the Palatinate and protect the inheritance of the heir to the English throne. The debate was long and heated, and, finally, the Hispanophiles and the pacifists combined to stymie the king. Instead of war finance,

Parliament voted 'a free gift of two entire subsidies', which amounted to about £140,000.[7] It was a pittance.

Bewildered by this opposition, the king was never able to understand its source. In truth it arose from a combination of motives, not all of them compatible. Hatred of Buckingham by those who had crossed him and been punished by loss of influence and office spurred some to oppose the king; others were angered that the promises made in 1624 were not kept. Many of the lawyers in the House were still looking for ways to assert the institutional power of Parliament that had been successfully repelled by James. The accession of a new monarch was another opportunity to refight old wars. Merchants continued to complain about impositions, the tax placed on luxury imports that had never been authorized by Parliament. Opposition to the cost of war weighed heavily on those who were against increased taxation, a solid block throughout the 1620s. With fear of the plague added to the mix, the parliament of 1625 was likely to go off the rails and lead to the wreckage of Charles's subsequent assemblies of his subjects.

Unable to absorb the shock of Parliament's refusal to provide separately for the war, the king sought to ameliorate the situation. With members fleeing London, his choices were to dissolve Parliament or prorogue it to reconvene at some place free of plague. Choosing the latter course, he summoned Parliament to meet in Oxford three weeks later. There Charles sought to assuage these concerns. He empowered Parliament to declare war and name the enemy; he sent Sir John Coke to lay out the naval estimates in unprecedented detail; and he appointed Viscount Wimbledon and the Earl of Essex admirals to lead the expedition, thereby placating those who opposed Buckingham. Still the Commons refused to grant funding, and when plague reached Oxford, the frenzy that had bedevilled the London session returned. Members were keener to criticize James and attack Buckingham than they were to back the war. Charles made a personal appeal, appearing before the two Houses and begging for aid: 'Better far it were both for your honours and mine that with hazard of half the fleet it were set forth than with assured loss of so much provision it were stayed home.'[8] Still the purse strings remained knotted. Worse, the Lower House took the opportunity of Charles's accession to re-evaluate royal customs revenue. Though every monarch since Henry VI had been voted to receive the import duties of tonnage and poundage for life, the Commons proposed granting it to Charles for only one year, and even this miserly proposal died silently in the Lords. Parliament was dissolved on 13 August.

Realistically, it was too late in the campaigning season to launch a successful fleet, but the king was intent on showing his mettle. Already armed and supplied, his flotilla was instructed to attack Spanish shipping and attempt the capture of the treasure ships laden with American gold. The campaign was a fiasco. Wimbledon, seizing the opportunity for military glory, made straight for the Spanish port of Cadiz, the site where Sir Walter Raleigh had triumphantly 'singed the King of Spain's beard'. But whereas Raleigh had led skilled and tested seamen, Wimbledon did not. The captains of the merchant ships that had been pressed into service refused to put their vessels in harm's way; Essex, arriving late on the scene, declined to give precedence and follow orders; and the winds, as always for Charles, were contrary. The returning fleet was scattered up and down the English coast with many ships sunk and many sailors drowned.

Domestic life was no easier than foreign affairs for the young king. His new French bride, Henrietta Maria – despite being a headstrong, emotional girl, 'full of spirit and vigour' – was terrified of the circumstances in which she found herself.[9] She spoke no English and learned slowly, further isolating herself from the court in which she lived. Buckingham, acting as equerry, attempted to instruct the newly-wed on how to be more affectionate. She was even more terrified of the over-sexed duke than she was of her persistent husband. Physically pained and emotionally fraught, torn between her attachment to her lifelong French companions and her duty to her husband, without reserves of education or experience on which to draw, Henrietta Maria contributed little to Charles's romantic expectation of wedded bliss.

Compounding the marital strife was the queen's personality. One of her first letters was an apology for 'my little sulky fit' and at her marriage she was still a mercurial teenager, given to giggling bouts and temper tantrums.[10] Unfortunately for Charles, his portion was of the latter. 'I suppose none but a Queen could cast such a scowl,' wrote one court watcher.[11] Nor did she fight fair. She denied her husband access to her bed and moped ostentatiously in his presence. She snubbed Buckingham's mother and wife by refusing to appoint Englishwomen in her household. More significantly, she declined to be crowned in a Protestant ceremony. Charles went to his coronation alone and the queen was never formally invested. Likewise, she declined to view the opening procession of the parliament of 1626. In June of that year, as if on a walk of penitence, Henrietta Maria knelt before the gallows at Tyburn where English Catholics had been executed. The king would brook no more. Charles personally informed his wife that her entourage was to be sent home. An extraordinary scene followed. Henrietta Maria raged at her husband and, spying her servants in the courtyard, broke windowpanes with her hands, crying out that she was being imprisoned. The king's resolve was firm. He ordered Buckingham: 'let me hear no answer but of the performance of my command . . . driv[e] them away like so many wild beasts'.[12] Within days, Charles had appointed a new court for his queen composed entirely of English officials.

Charles's troubles with his wife mirrored his deteriorating relationship with France. Little had come of the alliance to recover the Palatinate. Secret negotiations had led to a peace treaty between France and Spain, and the toleration guaranteed to the Huguenots was breached. La Rochelle, the stronghold of French Protestantism, was besieged partly by use of the very English ships lent to France for a promised campaign against Spain's ally, Genoa. Each action was a brazen French violation of the marriage terms and each was justified by counterclaims of English perfidy. Spitefully, the French revealed the secret clauses pertaining to the relaxation of anti-Catholic laws and accused Charles of failing to honour them. The expulsion of Henrietta Maria's Catholic servants caused the French to refuse to pay the second dowry instalment.

Hoping that his second parliament would achieve what his first had not, Charles did all he could to lay the groundwork for success. The anti-Catholic legislation passed in 1625 had been vigorously enforced; Catholic peers had been disarmed; and a number of Catholic councillors had been dismissed from office. Wimbledon's voyage, meanwhile, had served as an open declaration of war on Spain. To ease opposition, a number of obstructive MPs from the previous parliament were appointed as sheriffs, who were required to reside in their counties and were thus kept away from Westminster. Finally, the king kept his word on a promise made in 1625 that if Parliament voted him immediate subsidies, he would summon a second session to hear grievances.

The king's opening speech made no immediate request for war finance and for an entire month the Commons was given its head to form committees and ready bills. Then the king asked for supply. Although no specific amount was stated, the navy estimated its needs at £1 million, an impossible sum. But the escalating cost of war was not the real problem; many members of the Lower House were unwilling to fight at any price. Pleas from the House of Lords that supply be considered were rebuffed by complaints that 'no man will be willing to give his money into a bottomless gulf'.[13] The most the Lower House was willing to promise was that it 'would make your Majesty feared abroad and safe at home'.[14] This was a pledge that could not be used on the credit markets and it was followed by a more ominous declaration: 'it is better to die by an enemy than to suffer at home'.[15]

The grievances being churned out by multiple committees all coalesced in the resolution that the general cause of the kingdom's ills was the Duke of Buckingham. When the French illegally sequestered the English wine fleet, London merchants howled and blamed the Lord Admiral for their losses. When privateers attacked English shipping, traders blamed Buckingham's conduct of the war with Spain. The duke was even accused of allowing the French to use the loaned ships against La Rochelle, though in truth he had struggled mightily to prevent it. As friend, minister and favourite, Buckingham was the target for all of the criticism that could not be levelled at the monarch.

The Commons demanded that the king allow an impeachment of his admiral and chief adviser. Charles's initial inclination was to dissolve the parliament. But Buckingham dissuaded him, thinking he could easily demonstrate his innocence. Not wanting another campaigning season to dissipate into the mists of parliamentary procedure, Charles offered to take measures against the duke, presumably by relieving him of some of his many offices. After long debate the Commons rejected this solution and a formal impeachment began. Committees were appointed to draft charges and gather evidence. Among the most incendiary accusations was that Buckingham, perhaps with Charles's collusion, had poisoned James I during his final illness.

A persistent error in modern histories of Charles's relations with his parliaments is the claim that he dissolved the

1626 session to prevent Buckingham's impeachment. On the contrary, once Charles reluctantly allowed the proceedings to go forward, all he wished for was a speedy resolution. He sent message after message asking for haste; all were ignored. The Commons methodically drew up charges and presented the impeachment to the Lords. Though his opponents were able to impeach Buckingham, they were not able to convict him. The case was weak and he exploded it with scathing logic. The parliament had now lasted into June without the king acquiring his supply or the Commons the duke's scalp. The breaking point came when the Lower House, frustrated by its own legal ineptitude, demanded that, convicted or not, Buckingham be removed. To compound their attack, members voted it illegal for the crown to collect tonnage and poundage and listed impositions, another customs duty that the crown had collected since the reign of Queen Mary, as a grievance to be redressed before a vote of supply. There was nothing left for the king to do. Months before, he had offered to curtail Buckingham's powers. Now it was June and he was no further forward. Moreover, without revenue from impositions and tonnage and poundage, his government would simply collapse. He dissolved Parliament rather than receive the Commons remonstrance that would have beggared him.

No assembly of his subjects had a greater impact on Charles's attitude towards parliaments than that of 1626. The year before, the king had expected harmony; the year after, he was prepared for constant confrontation. The parliament of 1626 was the hinge on which an open door

swung shut. It stripped away all illusion that he would suc-
ceed where his father had failed. First he left the Commons
to its own devices, then he attempted to direct its business.
Both courses were equally fruitless. He ignored slights
spoken against his reputation and, when they continued, he
imprisoned the malefactors. 'As never king was more loving
to his people . . . so there was never king more jealous of his
honour,' he was led to proclaim in frustration.[16] Both
approaches recoiled on him. When he made concessions,
more were demanded; when he refused them, business
ground to a halt. He forbade the impeachment of the Duke
of Buckingham and the Commons pushed forward against
his will; he relented and it abandoned the botched impeachment. His pleas were met with silence, his admonitions with
remonstrance. In 1626, Charles lost whatever innocence he
may once have had regarding assemblies of his subjects.

Without money, Charles could not contribute to the
Protestant war effort. He had pledged aid to his uncle
Christian IV, the King of Denmark, and his failure to pay it
contributed to the Danish defeat that year at the Battle of
Lutter. The king was desperate to prevent the destruction of
the Huguenots at La Rochelle, but his fleet was only partially outfitted to resume the war against Spain. In 1626,
meetings of the Privy Council centred entirely on emergency revenue schemes and it was ultimately agreed to
demand a loan from his wealthier subjects. The king issued
a declaration laying the blame for the dissolution of Parliament squarely on those who had refused compromise, and
sent his officials into the counties to raise nearly a quarter

of a million pounds. The design, for which there was ample precedent, was a financial success and a political disaster. Though there were many motives for refusing, the one that struck the loudest chord was constitutional, that the loan violated the right of Englishmen to consent to taxation in Parliament. Technically, the loan was not a tax. It included provisions for repayment and was thus financially preferable to a subsidy. However, once the issue of rights was raised, it became clear that some were willing to sacrifice their purses for their principles. The crown could only think of its treasury. Many of those who had obstructed subsidies now obstructed the loan. The most vociferous were jailed and a lawsuit ensued that would have momentous implications in the future. But for the moment the loan replenished the king's coffers and his commanders staggered through another campaign. More Spanish and French ships were captured on the high seas, yet the Habsburg grip on the Palatinate only tightened.

In 1627, Charles risked everything to save his fellow Protestants, ensuring a diplomatic break between England and France. Dishonoured by the French use of English loan ships to crush a Huguenot flotilla, and angered by the detention of the Bordeaux wine fleet, Charles and Buckingham sought to relieve the Protestant stronghold of La Rochelle. The fleet despatched was underfunded and supplied with little else except the hopes of the king. It nearly won the day: Buckingham landed on the Ile de Ré – a strategic point for breaking the French blockade – and almost starved its garrison into submission. All he needed was resupply and reinforcement. He begged the king for aid and

Charles begged everyone he could for money. But neither was forthcoming. Charles described the expedition as 'happily begun, but, I must confess with grief, ill seconded'.[17] For this he blamed himself. Worse, the winds that had kept the French from resupplying the garrison now shifted, and Buckingham's advantage was lost. Soon it was the English who were imperilled. Their retreat became a rout. Unable to cross a narrow bridge to safety, the English troops were slaughtered. At least a thousand were killed in a single day. Nearly seven thousand men had embarked to Ile de Ré and barely half returned alive.

The king's plight was almost irretrievable. In order to secure the safety of Elizabeth, his sister and heir, he had risked relations with his wife and his subjects, had emptied his treasury and had endangered his favourite. Protestant forces on the continent had been routed and the siege of La Rochelle tightened. The only path out of his many predicaments was a successful parliament. Charles is often criticized for being simultaneously at war with the two greatest European powers, but both of those wars were offensive. England was never in danger from its enemies. No Spanish fleet menaced English shores and no French navy threatened English shipping. In fact, despite the overt military failures, the policy of privateering against both French and Spanish shipping had been a stunning success. The capture of French prizes along with the loan had funded Buckingham's initial convoy and Spanish ships were so vulnerable that they didn't dare to weigh anchor. Indeed, overtures for a peace with Spain were already in progress, though they were a long way from fruition. Nevertheless, another expedition against France needed an infusion of cash that only subsidies could bring. King and council decided to summon Parliament. Charles was willing to redress grievances, approve new laws and eliminate waste in his government. What he was not willing to do was endure either another attack on Buckingham or on his prerogatives. He made clear that if this parliament failed, it was likely to be his last.

For once, veteran leaders of the Commons shared the king's outlook. 'This is the crisis of parliaments; by this we shall know whether parliament will live or die.'[18] As much as they resented the unabated power of the duke, this was no longer their primary concern. Charles's ability to raise large amounts of money without parliamentary consent violated one of the most cherished beliefs Englishmen held about their liberties. Consent to taxation had been a principle laid down in Magna Carta in 1215 and confirmed by statute over the centuries. By compelling a loan, Charles had seemingly found a wedge against this immunity. When resistance appeared, the crown used its special powers of imprisonment to suppress it. In what became known as the Five Knights' Case against the loan resisters, the judges ruled that a man jailed by special command of the king had no relief from the common law. The lawyers howled in protest. Not only was a man's property unprotected from royal demand, his person was unsafe from royal incarceration. Charles could have his subsidies but only in return for a statement of the rights of Englishmen against such arbitrary actions of the crown, a Petition of Right.

As in 1626, Charles put up no resistance to the parliamentary inquiry into rights. He promised that if Parliament presented him with a bill to secure the liberties of the subject 'he [would] give way unto it'.[19] Again, he simply asked that the Commons despatch their business quickly so that he could prepare his fleet. The members did not share the royal sense of urgency. The Commons' leaders knew what they wanted, but were unclear how to get it. Should they proceed by bill or by petition? Should they simply ask for a reconfirmation of all statutes enshrining English liberties, or did they need to draw a new and more expansive one, a Magna Carta for the Stuart age? While they argued, Charles stewed. He placed no impediment to their proceedings other than to urge them to make a grant of supply. The Commons voted five subsidies, 'the greatest gift that ever any King of England had', but then bottled the bill up in committee while they proceeded with the Petition of Right.[20]

The problem was that the lawyers in the Commons insisted that the king had no power to imprison by special command and the judges and the Lords insisted that he did. This was an essential part of the royal prerogative and the king had promised to accept any bill or petition that did not touch his prerogative. They were in a maze without an apparent exit. Charles promised on the word of a king that he would never again confine by special command except in matters of national security, but the Commons wanted more than pledges. Their attempt to prepare a bill collapsed and instead they decided to proceed by petition. Anticipating the subsidies that were dangling before him, Charles launched the first part of his relief fleet, but then had to endure another month of legal wrangling. Finally, the

Petition of Right was concluded and Charles instantly granted it in the traditional manner. This did not satisfy the most vociferous critics of the crown. Though they had abandoned procedure by bill, they wanted the petition accepted as if it was a bill and they wanted it enrolled as if a statute. To force the king's hand, the MPs launched an attack on Buckingham. Charles was trapped and he meekly surrendered. But once the subsidy bill was passed, he quickly shifted his tone. 'I must tell you now that you do not understand so much as I thought you had done.'[21] Rather than receive the remonstrance against the duke and a prohibition on the collection of tonnage and poundage, Charles instantly prorogued the session.

His difficulties with Parliament were hardly at an end, but for the moment he had the money necessary to send a large relief force. The king himself went to Portsmouth to oversee the preparations. While there was still hope of peace between the King of France and his Protestant subjects, a well-armed flotilla might be a persuasive argument in itself. Buckingham followed Charles, resolved to command the fleet in person. On 23 August as the duke rose from breakfast, he was stabbed to death. His assailant, John Felton, a soldier aggrieved over his pay, emboldened by the broadsheets and pamphlets that had vilified Buckingham, viewed himself as a courageous Brutus. He purchased a tenpenny knife in a Portsmouth shop, walked up to the duke and plunged it into him. He would have escaped had he not pronounced himself the perpetrator. Buckingham's entourage looked on in such consternation that no one thought to run the assassin through. Felton's public execution was a final occasion for those who hated the duke to express their hostility.

Charles was devastated by the death of his best friend. Negotiations in France and war in Germany depended on missions that Buckingham had organized. For the moment, royal policy collapsed into disarray. Charles's confident bellicosity died with the duke. Buckingham had buoyed his spirits when things had gone wrong and was ever optimistic about the future. Gradually, the king began to make more peaceable overtures to both France and Spain. Louis promised to grant his Protestant subjects freedom of worship if they surrendered to him and pledged peace. Negotiations with Spain made equal progress. England's participation in the Thirty Years War thus came to a quiet end.

The king had only one more piece of unfinished business, the prorogued parliamentary session. With the duke gone, there should not have been any obstacle to providing Charles with tonnage and poundage and ending the controversy over illegal taxation. But where the king wished to settle financial matters, the Commons wished to settle religious ones. Religious grievance, long simmering beneath the constitutional struggles of the decade, now spilled over. Charles was a pious Protestant, but his version of Anglicanism tended towards the formal, the ceremonial and the liturgical. He had deep respect for the authority of bishops. To many of his 'hotter Protestant' subjects, the king's style of piety was reminiscent of Roman Catholic 'idolatry'. Contention over Charles's choice of bishops, over prosecution of his religious critics and over a complex theological dispute about predestination dominated the session. The bill for collection of tonnage and poundage was sent to committee, while the Commons waded into the turbulent waters of religious grievances. This was an area where the king had high confidence in his own opinions, and a high regard for his own authority. When Charles attempted to adjourn the session on 2 March 1629, pandemonium ensued. Some of the rasher members locked the door to the House and forcibly pinned the Speaker to his chair. With the session thus prolonged, the chaotic House adopted resolutions on religion and against the collection of tonnage and poundage.

The king lost little time in responding. Parliament was dissolved, nine members of the Commons were imprisoned and a royal proclamation stated what was now only too evident: 'we shall account it presumption for any to prescribe any time unto us for parliaments'.[22] Charles I had had his fill of parliaments. It would be eleven years before another was summoned.

3
Peace and Prosperity

Peace with France in 1629 and with Spain a year later ended the tumultuous opening of the king's reign. He had learned bitter lessons and had swallowed bitter pills. His promises to aid his sister, his Danish uncle and the French Huguenots had all been broken. His desire to make England a feared and respected nation had been dashed. He had clashed with his subjects in each of his parliaments and his relations with his assemblies were in shambles after the 1629 riot in the House of Commons. Charles's public declaration that he would call no more sessions was matched by his private sentiment. As he told the Earl of Dorset, he resolved 'not to come to parliament in necessity or upon necessity'.[1] There was little left for him to do but make peace. Fortunately neither of his two European foes had the inclination to enforce punitive treaties. The French said nothing of easing Catholic persecution and the Spanish demanded no reparations for the loss of their shipping. Both could foresee a time when they would need English aid. Charles, who never abandoned his ambitions, licked his wounds and waited.

Peace with his brother-in-law presaged peace with his wife. The difficult early days of their marriage were made no easier while England was at war with France, but Henrietta Maria, whom Charles always called Mary or addressed as *cher cœur*, turned her attention to pleasing her husband. Since the death of Buckingham, king and queen had grown closer. After years of bickering, Charles could report to his mother-in-law, Marie de' Medici: 'the only dispute that now exists between us is that of conquering each other by affection'.[2] They were constantly together and courtiers witnessed frequent public displays of affection. The queen's miscarriage in 1629 was a blow to Charles, but when he instructed the doctors to save the mother – 'the mould rather than the cast' – he made a profound statement of his love.[3] She learned English well enough to perform in a court masque for Charles's birthday in 1633. Her French tastes blazed the fashion trends of the court, and she hired troops of decorators, artists and cabinetmakers to refurbish her palaces. She utilized French cooks and planted gardens in the French style. Charles delighted in giving her gifts of imported fruits and vegetables. The masques she sponsored were all variations on the theme of Platonic love, though her feelings for her husband were conceived differently. In rapid succession she gave birth to two princes, Charles (1630) and James (1633), both of whom would rule as English kings. She had nine pregnancies in fifteen years and doted on her family. 'I had every pleasure the heart could desire; I had a husband who adored me.'[4]

Moreover, with descendants of his own body, Charles's obsession with the fate of his sister and brother-in-law eased. The Palatine pair were no longer his direct heirs and their safety and restoration no longer urgent British problems. Though Charles would continue his financial support, it was not long before his gaze turned inward to the establishment of domestic order and pursuit of prosperity. The conclusion of war with France and Spain that had been forced upon him by penury now became the blessings of peace so praised by his father. The poet Thomas Carew dubbed the 1630s 'our halcyon days' and the Earl of Clarendon recalled how the nation 'enjoyed the greatest calm and the fullest measure of felicity, that any people in any age . . . have been blessed with'.[5]

Charles's own domestic activities were expressive of that felicity. Household servants reported the king's overflowing affection towards his children. He named the first navy ships built during his reign after his sons. He hung their portraits in his private chamber and oversaw their upbringing with a degree of attention unusual for a king. Despite the terms of the marriage treaty, the Protestant Countess of Dorset and Earl of Newcastle were placed in charge of Prince Charles. The Calvinist Brian Duppa tutored him and his brother James in religion. The king insisted on a strict separation between the public and private spaces occupied by the royal family. The household was walled off from the court and rules were established to regulate access to the king. Whether his taste for organization was a reaction against the disarray of his father's court or admiration for the formality he had witnessed in Spain, he insisted that his regulations be strictly observed. Charles was fastidious, but he was not fussy. He followed a daily routine, waking punctually each morning, attending prayers and keeping to a schedule of business. He ended each day by winding his pocket watch. This was not, as some have supposed, an obsessive compulsion, but rather the comfort of habit. When circumstances demanded, the king could be flexible and spontaneous.

He also could enjoy himself. His chief sport was hunting, pursued vigorously through forest and fields. Royal hunting lodges were scattered over south-eastern England, though the one at Newmarket was his favourite. When not antici-pating or recovering from childbirth, the queen joined the hunts. Charles also collected art. Nothing gave him greater pleasure during this period than his growing collection. When art shipments arrived, he would hurry to open them like a child on Christmas morning and would examine them inch by inch. His greatest coup was the purchase of the collection of the dukes of Mantua, which included masterpieces by Raphael, Titian and Correggio. The king had a genuine appreciation for quality and could distin-guish the work of masters from those of their apprentices. He brought to his court the Flemish painters Rubens and Van Dyck, whom he knighted and commissioned to pro-vide a visual record of royal and aristocratic life in the Caroline age. The king accumulated nearly 1,800 paintings and over 500 ancient sculptures, one of the most substan-tial of all royal collections in history.

Charles was not simply an aesthete. He understood the political power of images. He had dynastic portraits made of his grandmother, Mary, Queen of Scots, and of his sister, Elizabeth. One of Van Dyck's most powerful depictions of Charles's imperial aspirations showed the king making an entry through a Roman triumphal arch. A picture of the king in armour was placed in public rooms at the end of a row of Roman emperors. The message was unmistakable.

But in many respects, imagery aside, Charles had left behind his youthful thirst for global grandeur. Royal government in the 1630s instead revolved around a drive for efficiencies and reform. After Buckingham's death, Charles never again elevated a favourite. Buckingham had insulated Charles, but his dependency on the duke had made him vulnerable. Instead, Charles made greater use of the Privy Council, whose membership expanded and was divided into committees. It was a group with diverse opinions and outlooks, chiefly composed of astute politicians with a finger in the wind. The king brought many of his parliamentary critics into government once they showed themselves willing to serve. Charles took advice from his councillors and considered issues from many perspectives. It is perhaps a tribute to his style of governing that half of his modern critics believe he was too easily swayed by his councillors, while the other half believe he too frequently ignored their advice. The most important royal minister during the 1630s was the Lord Treasurer, Sir Richard Weston, Earl of Portland. Weston had been a friend and client of the Earl of Middlesex, who had served James in the same role. Middlesex had famously instituted economies for a notoriously uneconomical king, even going so far as to reduce the court allowance for candles. Weston was similarly moulded. In a few years he had managed to pay off Charles's war debts and to increase his revenue by nearly £50,000.

Charles's government aspired to extend central control into the localities. In 1631 the Privy Council issued the Book of Orders to justices of the peace, in a partially successful attempt to standardize the work of county justices and to make better provisions for the poor. At the same time, the king ordered the gentry to leave London and reside in their counties so as to fulfil their duties as governors. Local government depended on the physical presence of the worthies of each county. The lure of the capital, however, meant that such proclamations were required on an annual basis. Other efforts to improve governance stemmed directly from Charles's own interests. Although he could not afford it, he never abandoned his desire to re-enter the European war. To prepare better for this eventuality, the council issued orders to create an 'exact militia'. The ramshackle trained bands of England's counties were thus to be introduced to the modern drilling methods pioneered on the continent. Military manuals were despatched to aid the deputy-lieutenants in their tasks of assembling and arming able-bodied men. Experienced soldiers were hired as muster masters to whip them into shape. High constables did the administrative work and sent muster rolls to London so that the council's military committees could have a full record of local activity. Like the Book of Orders, the Exact Militia was more effectively planned than executed. Local government in early modern England depended on the unpaid efforts of social elites, and where their local prestige conflicted with the royal will, the former tended to prevail. Nevertheless, Charles achieved a level of military preparedness hitherto unknown.

The king's real military passion was in the navy. He learned much about naval affairs from Buckingham, whom he never replaced as Lord Admiral, the office devolving on his second son, James. He personally inspected ships and sailors at the naval yards, famously descending into their holds to discover if they were seaworthy. England was entering its first great age of shipbuilding and Charles was determined to create a fighting fleet less dependent upon the hiring of merchantmen. During the 1630s, he had eleven new ships of the line built, including the mammoth thousand-ton, hundred-gun *Sovereign of the Seas*, the largest fighting ship yet constructed. Defence of the Channel was essential to English trade. Constituting the only neutral sea power of the decade, English ships were hired by the French to convoy their wine fleets and by the Spanish to protect their silver-laden flotillas. They also dominated the re-export trade, lading goods destined to Antwerp or Amsterdam. The port of Dover became a new entrepôt, drawing a flood of customs duties that helped defray the cost of shipbuilding. But English ships were also rich targets for the ever-present pirates that plied the same sea lanes. The Dunkirkers, who operated with impunity from the Spanish Netherlands, captured or destroyed over sixty English merchantmen annually and that number increased once France declared war against the Habsburgs in 1635. Worse were the Salé pirates from Morocco, who not only plundered cargoes but also captured and sold sailors into slavery, and even raided English port towns for slaves. Charles's enhanced navy had to be constantly vigilant to defend the Channel – and vigilance was expensive.

Initially, the king funded his shipbuilding from his own revenues. But the cost of setting forth annual fleets was beyond royal income. It was necessary to find another source of revenue, one that could be exploited without parliamentary approval. Charles had agreed not to tax his subjects without consent and throughout the 1630s his finance ministers had been reviving long-disused prerogative revenues. Knighthood fines were assessed on those who had not purchased the honour when Charles's eldest son was born. Forest encroachers were fined even when the land they occupied had become pasture devoid of timber. Customs duties were raised, especially on imported luxury goods. All of these schemes allowed the king to remain solvent but they did not solve his larger problem. Nor were they popular. Though they were conventional ways by which the crown had raised money in the past, they revived concern that Charles was violating the spirit, if not the letter, of the Petition of Right.

In 1633 discussions began in the Privy Council for the revival of ship money, a military charge used in times of emergency. Ship money was originally a levy of vessels in an era when there was no standing royal navy. Warrants were issued to all of the coastal and port towns either to provide ships or their money equivalent. Because ship money was paid directly to the treasurers of the navy, the king's legal councillors concluded that it was a levy rather than a tax and therefore did not violate the Petition of Right. Writs were issued in 1634 following the traditional form of rating only the coastal areas. These did not yield enough revenue to outfit ships in sufficient numbers to protect the Channel.

In 1635, after another consultation with the judges, writs were extended to the kingdom at large. The demand was given teeth by authorizing sheriffs to seize the property of defaulters. Ship money was no hastily devised scheme. It had been debated in the Privy Council, researched by the law officers, and twice approved hypothetically by all of the judges. Charles had every reason to believe that he was on solid ground in instituting the levy.

As a source of revenue, ship money proved effective. It paid for an annual fleet that protected English shipping and defended the narrow seas from marauders. But as a political measure, it was resented on both practical and constitutional grounds. Places that had never before paid ship money objected to a new levy from which they only received a theoretical benefit. Those who had struggled in Parliament for the absolute protection of property believed the new levy violated the rights of Englishmen. Like the loan in 1626, it straddled the line between legality and abuse. In 1637, John Hampden, a gentleman living in landlocked Buckinghamshire, refused to pay his assessment and sued the sheriff for confiscating an equivalent amount of his goods. The case challenged monarchical prerogative at several levels: was the king sole arbiter of national defence; did he alone determine when the nation was in danger; and when he had so determined, did he have the right to demand levies from his subjects? The judges were fundamentally agreed on these constitutional questions, and favourable to the royal position. But the extension of the levy to inland communities raised issues of precedent rather than principle. Though ten of the twelve judges found against

Hampden on the constitutional issues, five found in his favour on the specifics of the writ. Ship money was declared legal, but the partial vindication of Hampden fuelled sporadic resistance and hot discontent.

Another, still more inflammatory source of discontent simmered throughout the 1630s: religion. For generations, some people had regarded the English Reformation as incomplete, an unsteady achievement compromised by the idiosyncratic religious preferences of Queen Elizabeth and King James. On an axis running between Catholic Rome and Calvinist Geneva, they viewed the Church of England as leaning too far towards the Roman pole. Its theology was too sacramental, its liturgy too ceremonial. Many strict Calvinists disdained such 'high' practices as kneeling for communion or bowing at every mention of Jesus's name. Most of all they hated the continued presence of bishops in the government of the English Church long after they had been abolished in the Calvinist churches.

Dissatisfaction with the Caroline Church began among ministers and gradually spread to the 'hot reformers' among the laity. These latter regarded themselves as the 'godly' or the 'elect'. Others regarded them as disobedient upstarts and referred to them, derisively, as Puritans. The name Puritan was an umbrella under which sheltered a range of religious dissidents, most of them in fact rather moderate critics who wished to reform the Church from within. But among the Puritans were also a small group of 'separatists' who wished to uproot the national Church and replace it with an alternative organized either as a Presbyterian or a congregational system.

Puritans had only one thing in common, a visceral hatred of popery. They were quick to taint their opponents with this and, as the decades passed, many local communities engaged in a culture war over religion. Some of those Puritans who despaired of reforming Charles's Church from within accepted voluntary exile, first in Holland and then in New England. The flood of families and ministers traversing the Atlantic came to be known as the Great Migration. They left, as one of them recorded, to escape 'the multitude of irreligious, lascivious and popishly affected persons' among whom they found themselves living.[6] Most settled in Massachusetts Bay. Between 1630 and 1642, perhaps as many as fifteen thousand made the journey to establish a city on a hill, a religious beacon to point the way for their English brethren.

But most Puritans remained in England to battle for the soul of the Caroline Church. Religious discontent, particularly over points of doctrine, had roiled all of Charles's parliaments. A particular flashpoint had been the writings of the clergyman Richard Montague, who blithely sought to minimize the doctrinal differences between Catholic and Protestant beliefs. Though James (who fancied himself a royal theologian) had declared Montague's views orthodox, Charles's parliaments wanted them suppressed. The king's first attempt to defuse this landmine was to make Montague a royal chaplain and therefore beyond reach of a parliamentary investigation. His second attempt was an effort at compromise. He convened a meeting at York House of those who supported Montague – Arminians, in contemporary parlance – and those Calvinists who opposed him. Nothing was settled.

Meanwhile, the rise of English Arminianism (named after a celebrity Dutch theologian called Jacob Arminius) galvanized Puritan suspicion. Calvinists believed in double predestination: that individual salvation and damnation were absolute judgements determined by God according to an inscrutable divine plan. Arminius countered this austere theology by positing that the saved could fall away from grace through their own failures. He thereby introduced an element of human free will into predestination. Free will was a Catholic doctrine and thus Arminians were accused of a crypto-Romanism. Unfortunately, the Thirty-Nine Articles, which formed the doctrinal constitution of the English Church, were ambiguous on these points. For three generations, Calvinists attempted to amend them with an explicit affirmation of double predestination, and they failed every time. Insistence on the irretrievable damnation of the majority was an uncomfortable social doctrine for both Church and state, as it induced at best despair and at worst lawlessness. In 1628, in a reissue of the Thirty-Nine Articles, the king prohibited all discussion of predestination. Montague's publications were withdrawn and enforcement of this ban was impartial. But to Calvinists who believed that they were defending orthodoxy, such 'evenhandedness' looked like a dangerous indulgence of heresy. Unlicensed publications attacking Arminianism proliferated. The royal prerogative courts of High Commission and Star Chamber were compelled to act as censors.

While the king attempted to steer a middle ground in the conflict over predestination, he would not indulge attacks upon episcopacy. Archbishops and bishops, who maintained orthodoxy in their dioceses, administered the English Church as ecclesiastical princes. Unlike many Catholic bishops, English bishops were almost never aristocrats. But distinguished university careers and stints as royal chaplains compensated for their modest origins. Charles's episcopal appointments followed patterns established by his father and it is difficult to discern the imposition by the king of any doctrinal test for preferment. The bench of bishops was as divided over the question of absolute predestination as were the theologians. Most agreed with Archbishop William Laud's assessment that 'something about these controversies is unmasterable in this life'.[7]

Laud became Archbishop of Canterbury in 1633, and found himself at the eye of the storm. He was temperamentally at one with the king. Like his master, he was an educated and introspective man (he kept a dream diary), though his collecting tastes ran to rare manuscripts rather than artworks. Both wished to damp down controversies and both insisted upon maintaining order. Laud had come into favour a decade earlier when he prevented the scandalous possibility of Buckingham's mother converting to Catholicism and he rose rapidly through the clerical ranks. He was an institutional man and his principal objective was to protect the wealth and the prerogatives of the Church from the ever-present jealousies of the English gentry. Laud closed down a London corporation that was buying up Church livings that eluded the jurisdiction of the bishops; he attacked freelancing urban lecturers because they did not catechize. For him a church was a sacred space to be treated with reverence, a vessel containing the 'beauty of holiness'.[8] Though his critics believed Laud an all-powerful ecclesiastical despot in the manner of a Protestant pope, he was in fact a cautious man who rarely acted without explicit direction from the king. Nor did he always get his way in the king's counsels. An obscure but hotly contested controversy over the placement of the communion table within churches was resolved in a typical royal compromise much to Laud's frustration. Laud's desire to import the English prayer book into the Church of Scotland was ignored.

Because it was impossible to criticize the king directly, and in the absence of a favourite to replace Buckingham, it was the bishops who became the targets of agitation. In some dioceses, the bishop was mostly a ceremonial figure and supervision of the clergy was lax. In others, especially those with large concentrations of Puritans, activist bishops stirred the pot, summoning ministers for examination and occasionally suspending them when they refused to conform. Each instance of ecclesiastical discipline was magnified within the godly community, which came to believe, quite dubiously, that Laud and his minions had unleashed a reign of terror against them. The standard instrument of conformity was a diocesan visitation in which bishops heard complaints against wayward parishioners and ministers. More serious breaches came before the Court of High Commission, where Archbishop Laud himself sat in judgement.

Charles made few statements that revealed his personal beliefs. He was pious and attended the entire weekday liturgical service, unlike his father, who had usually come only for the sermon. But his views remain masked, giving rise to much speculation. Those who think he favoured Arminians emphasize the appointment of Richard Neale and Laud as archbishops. Those who believe he was a conventional Calvinist point to the fact that he attempted to bring the great Puritan preacher John Preston into his government. He consistently spoke in support of the Church as it had existed in Queen Elizabeth's time, which endeared him to neither of the extreme parties. When he reissued the Thirty-Nine Articles, he directed that they be interpreted according to the clear and unadorned meaning of their words. He stated on several occasions that he opposed all innovation in religion, though perforce only he could interpret what 'innovation' meant. Despite wild accusations, Charles was never attracted to Catholicism. He enforced the anti-Catholic laws more consistently than either Elizabeth or James, partly because he needed the fines they yielded but also partly because non-conformity was against the law. The king was genuinely appalled when his court was rocked by a number of high-profile female conversions to Rome and he responded by prohibiting English subjects from attending the queen's Catholic Masses. Although he refused to execute proselytizing priests, he had no hesitation in exiling them.

But Charles believed Puritans to be as much a danger to the Church and state as Catholics; in the 1630s restraining them became more of a challenge. They set themselves apart by their dress and demeanour and followed a rigid social code. In the early decades of the movement, Puritanism focused on the salvation of the saints, but as time passed they became equally concerned with chastisement of the damned. Thus it was not enough for the godly to observe strictly the Sabbath themselves; they now insisted on imposing such observance on their neighbours. Puritans believed that the Sabbath was reserved for worship, soul-searching and prayer. Most of their countrymen alloyed such piety with a spot of drinking or sport. When some Puritan magistrates attempted to prohibit Sunday pastimes, Charles intervened. He instructed that every minister read to their congregations the Book of Sports that defined lawful Sabbath activities. Despite the fact that Charles's Book of Sports was identical to the one issued by his father, Puritans were roused to fury against it. Puritan moralists opposed dancing, church music and, above all, stage plays. As theatre was one of the king's great pleasures – he patronized a troupe of actors and participated in court masques – assaults on the theatre came perilously close to attacks on the king. In 1633 the Lincoln's Inn lawyer William Prynne set new standards of vituperation in his book *Histrio-Mastix*, which condemned what he deemed pagan frivolities, including the viewing of stage plays. He compared the king to the Roman tyrant Nero and suggested that a number of ancient emperors had been justly assassinated for sponsoring or viewing plays. Most provocatively, he wrote that actresses were 'notorious whores' at a time when the queen was rehearsing to appear in a masque. Prynne was hauled before Star Chamber and after a long hearing was convicted of sedition. He was fined, pilloried and mutilated by the removal of his ears. His punishment sent shock waves through the Puritan community, especially when it was followed, three years later, by a second conviction and another mutilation. On this second occasion, Prynne shared the dock with co-defendants who had written explicitly anti-episcopal tracts attacking Archbishop Laud among other bishops as agents of the pope. The public punishment of these men attracted crowds estimated to be in the thousands, who hailed the convicts as martyrs to a cause of conscience. By the end of the decade, radical Puritanism was entering the mainstream.

4
Ireland and Scotland

Charles I ruled over three distinct kingdoms. England (since 1542 united with Wales) was a prosperous and settled nation, integrated into the European state system. Scotland, on the other hand, was a poor nation with few natural advantages. Agriculture was difficult on its rocky soil and its access to the sea was through treacherous waters and tempestuous gales. Then there was Ireland: if the Scottish were poor, the Irish were destitute, incapable even of defraying the costs of their own administration. The Irish, a conquered people, had been overrun by the Normans in the twelfth century and governed by the kings of England thereafter.

As independent kingdoms, Scotland and England had been ancient enemies. Prior to James VI and I, the three previous Scottish monarchs had died by English hands, either on the battlefield or the scaffold. The Scots' natural ally was France and James's mother, Mary, had been married to a French king. Where the Scots had allied with England's ancient enemy, the Irish inclined towards its modern one. During Elizabeth's reign, Irish leaders offered their crown to Philip II of Spain.

The political challenges posed by Charles's multiple monarchy were not its greatest ones, however. All three kingdoms contained a volatile combination of incompatible religions and each contained them in a different dominant mixture. England was a Protestant state with Catholic and Puritan fringes. The Puritans were vocally anti-Catholic, while the Catholics, though largely powerless, enjoyed the protection of international opinion. Scotland was predominantly a Puritan nation, with a Presbyterian Kirk that claimed independence from the crown. To assert royal control, James had planted bishops into the Scottish Church and ordered the creation of new canons and a prayer book. His reforms reflected the practices of mainstream English Protestants, and aspired towards an eventual unification of the English and Scottish Churches. Numerous kirk ministers were outspoken in opposition, contemptuous of the episcopal veneer that the Stuarts had tacked on to their sacrosanct Presbyterian Church. This contest between radical and moderate Protestants obscured the fact that Scotland also contained a sizable and powerful population of Roman Catholics, many of them the semi-autonomous Highland lords who barely accepted royal rule.

Ireland's religious mix was the mirror image of England's. Here the majority of the population was Catholic. The Church of Ireland, an English Protestant import, existed only in those areas under direct military control, though its members held a monopoly on political and legal power. Fewer still were the Scots Presbyterians who had emigrated to Ireland in James's reign to settle in Ulster. Like the English Puritans, they were fervently anti-Catholic, their fears only heightened by the seething discontent of the Catholic majority all around them. Given this constellation of religious allegiances, any Caroline religious policy was bound to be unpopular somewhere.

In Ireland, a military presence and the plantation, or settlement, of Protestants on formerly Catholic lands maintained effective government. James governed the Emerald Isle with measured brutality. His Lords Deputy enforced punitive anti-Catholic laws while doing everything possible to encourage a growing settler community. Dating back to Tudor times, the policy of plantation was designed to 'civilize' rebellious Ireland by imposing Protestantism and stifling tradition, Irish language, customary laws and clan networks. Though Catholics had few political rights, they dominated the Irish parliament until James created over eighty new seats, all located in the new Protestant areas. Ireland became a Catholic majority ruled by a Protestant minority. The Irish population was divided into three: the native Gaelic Catholics who comprised the largest number; the Catholic old English, descended from the families who had administered Ireland before the Protestant Reformation; and the Protestant new English, many of them actually Scots who were planted on lands more recently seized. Nearly a hundred thousand Protestants settled on Irish land during the reigns of Elizabeth and James. James's plantations in Munster had come at the expense of the old English, who had acted as brokers for their Gaelic co-religionists and owned half the land in rich south-eastern Ireland. As his reign progressed, they became alienated from the crown. Effective English control and defence of Dublin and its surrounds, an area known as the Pale, was maintained only by military force. Everywhere else, might was deemed right. Some dispossessed Catholics ached to have their lands restored and small bands of brigands occasionally beset Protestant settlements. There were no overt rebellions against James's Irish government but grievances accumulated.

Charles was least absorbed in the affairs of his conquered dominion. He never visited Ireland and was content to allow his Lords Deputy to exercise autonomous power. At the beginning of his reign, Ireland was a concern for it posed a security risk in the war against Spain as a potential staging ground for an invasion of England. It was necessary to enlarge the army and to station warships in Irish waters, increasing the costs of administration. These could only be afforded by raising taxes, especially upon the wealthy old English. In 1628 their leaders proposed to Charles a series of reforms in return for a large monetary grant. Known as the Graces, these redressed an array of Catholic complaints. The two most important concerned security of land tenure and the substitution of an oath of loyalty for the Protestant oath of supremacy. These would give Catholics clear legal title to their estates and allow them to hold public offices, affirming their allegiance to their king and their Church. In the end, the tax was paid but the Graces were not granted. Though the new English settlers and the bishops of the Church of Ireland were strongly opposed to concessions made to Catholics, Charles had determined to keep his bargain and grant the Graces. However, circumstances conspired to prevent this. Only an Irish parliament could validate the Graces and after the one summoned for

1628 was cancelled on a technicality, none was called until 1634. By that time, Charles had replaced a series of ineffectual Lords Deputy with Sir Thomas Wentworth, ultimately Earl of Strafford, who had a vision for governing Ireland.

Wentworth arrived in Ireland in 1633 with a programme to make Ireland fiscally stable by eliminating its annual deficit and paying down its accumulated debt. He recognized that this could not be done simply by fining Catholics and he set out to make the new English pay their share. In the Irish parliament of 1634, Wentworth pushed through an enhanced subsidy by promising old English members reconsideration of the Graces and new English representatives additional military protection. In all he raised nearly £300,000, twice what had been granted in the 1620s. But Strafford reneged on his promise to the old English, allowing the least contentious of the Graces to be presented to Parliament but baulking at security of land tenure and the oath of loyalty. There was simply too much opposition from the Protestant planters, and indeed Strafford had plans for expanding the hated plantations. He believed that only augmented Protestant settlements could stabilize Ireland, and expanding the plantations required that the crown confiscate land occupied by the old English. Thus he opposed their security of land tenure. But he also accepted that, during the long, slow march to a Protestant and 'civilized' Ireland, de facto toleration for Catholics was a necessary expedient. The Dublin government was too weak to attempt a policy of repression – 'as a man going to warfare without munitions or arms' – and too poor to carry one out had the attempt been made.[1]

Instead, Wentworth supported the expansion of the beleaguered Church of Ireland, hoping that this would support the new Protestant communities. He encouraged the bishops to reclaim Church lands that had been illegally confiscated and he set up commissions to end collusive rental agreements that impoverished the dioceses. In many bishoprics, annual income doubled. Unfortunately, balancing the bishops' books came at the expense of many new English settlers, who had fattened their own ledgers with what were by law Church revenues. Strafford used the legal machinery of the Lieutenancy, of which he was deputy, to restore these lands to the Church, stepping on the toes of some of the most powerful Protestant Irish landlords in the process. He had wisely secured a guarantee from Charles that no appeal of his decisions would be heard in London, but this meant that there was no outlet for the venting of opposition. Pressure began to build. By 1638, Strafford had alienated the old English by his refusing the Graces and the continued plantation of Protestants on their lands, and the new English through his taxes and the repatriation of Church estates. Groups bitterly opposed to each other had found a common enemy. Soon they would find a potential ally across the North Channel in Scotland.

Charles was born in Scotland, tutored by Scots and spoke with a Scottish inflection all his life. In every other way, he was English. He was also Scotland's first absentee monarch. His father bragged that he was able to rule Scotland by his pen, though that was after decades of face-to-face government. Charles had no such experience and his father's failure to achieve an incorporative union left him monarch of a separate kingdom with its own laws, customs and religion. Scottish politics were intensely internecine. Clan rivalries were interlaced with religious divisions, turf battles and age-old vendettas. With the centre of power and patronage now in London, ambitious Scots sought to renegotiate the terms of monarchy. Charles adamantly adhered to the constitutional practices he had inherited. Among his first acts was to reissue the Five Articles of Perth, James's ceremonial reforms that were hated within the Kirk. Charles had had two long deathbed conversations with his father and, in both, Scotland had been a central subject.

James also likely advised his son to keep the administration of his kingdoms separate. A Scottish privy council composed entirely of Scots sat in Edinburgh with a Scottish secretary who communicated directly with the king; a Scottish advocate advised Charles on legal matters; and John Spottiswood, Archbishop of St Andrews and ultimately Lord Chancellor, combined the highest offices in state and Church. No Englishman played any role in Scottish affairs and Charles suffered the misfortune that his father's most trusted Scottish adviser, the Marquess of Hamilton, died weeks before his accession. He relied first on the Earl of Menteith and later on the Earl of Traquair to guide his Scottish government. Both were effective and reasonably trustworthy.

Though preoccupation with his European wars prevented Charles from travelling north for a coronation, his advisers persuaded him to issue immediately an Act of Revocation. This was a legal device that allowed the crown to investigate titles of all lands acquired during a monarch's minority and revoke them if necessary. Since Scotland had a long history of royal minorities, and an even longer one of nobles feeding at the unprotected royal trough, revocations had followed the accession of each new monarch. Charles had had no actual minority in Scotland, as he came to the throne just months shy of his twenty-fifth birthday. But he was entitled to demand an inquiry into lands acquired during the minority of any of his predecessors, and this he did. While it is unclear as to who advised and drafted this document, and its legal technicalities were well beyond the ken of the king, he would later be challenged to defend them. Charles's Revocation differed little in practice from those of his predecessors, but his absentee status made landowners fearful that it would be carried out to the letter. In fact, since the commissions of inquiry were stacked with the malefactors they were supposed to pursue, very little land ever had been repatriated to the crown. This was precisely the case in Charles's reign, although there were constant complaints about what might happen rather than what did happen. Nevertheless, the Revocation did little to increase the popularity of an alien king.

When Charles was ready to make his coronation visit in 1631, the Scots were not prepared to receive him. The event took place in 1633 in the royal chapel at Holyrood Palace amid much splendour, to the chagrin of the more rigid Presbyterians who cavilled at the vestments worn by the bishops and the English prayer book used in the service. The parliament that followed was equally successful and the king personally attended the session. Two issues proved contentious, an increase in tax rates and the regulation of clerical dress, but both were extensions of his father's policies rather than his own innovations. The Act of Revocation passed without comment. A large English entourage accompanied Charles north, including Archbishop Laud, who assiduously investigated the state of the Scottish Kirk. He found everything in disarray, from badly maintained buildings, to undisciplined ministers, to vocally independent congregations. Services differed from parish to parish with no apparent uniformity and there was no standard Scottish prayer book, despite directions given in 1616 at the General Assembly in Aberdeen that one be prepared.

A committee composed entirely of Scottish churchmen had been assigned to draft a new prayer book but the work had never been finished. After Charles's visit, the committee was encouraged to complete it. Despite subsequent allegations, Laud opposed this process. He wanted the king to impose the English prayer book on the Kirk, thereby bringing the two Churches into liturgical uniformity. But Charles was determined to allow the Scots a measure of self-government, 'that it might truly and justly be reputed a book of that church's own composing'.[2] A committee led by Archbishop Spottiswood composed the book and circulated it among leading Scottish clergymen. The amended text was then sent to England where the king himself annotated it. In essence it was an attempt to order the Scottish service and to standardize it. Very little of its content was flagrantly 'English' in flavour, but what could be so identified was bitterly opposed. Laud had cautioned Spottiswood to secure widespread support before introducing the book – 'to be very careful what they did and how they demeaned themselves' – but Spottiswood believed that the consent of the bishops would encompass the consent of the Church.[3] This presumption of definitive episcopal authority was a fundamental miscalculation.

The controversy over the prayer book embroiled Charles in a crisis he had neither anticipated nor intended. Rumours circulated for weeks as to the content of the new service and the hotter-headed cohorts of Scottish Presbyterians began to organize protests in anticipation of its introduction. When, at the end of July 1637, the Dean of St Giles Church in Edinburgh began reading from the prayer book, a riot erupted. He was forced from the pulpit by a barrage of sticks and stones and milking stools and then assaulted as he made a narrow escape. This mob violence, an unthinkable violation of both sanctity and ecclesiastical rank, might well have proven lethal. To worsen matters, the Scottish privy council and the city authorities in Edinburgh either misunderstood the nature of the disturbance or were unwilling to admit that matters had spiralled out of control. They reported to Charles that the riot was the work of ignorant, 'base and rascal people'. Charles ordered that it be suppressed with appropriate rigour.[4] He also instructed the privy council to provide security for those ministers introducing the prayer book. These orders, based on misinformation, in any case arrived in Edinburgh too late. It was by then apparent that this was not a mob riot but a carefully orchestrated resistance movement. Its leaders were not rowdy milkmaids but a cadre of kirk ministers opposed to the ecclesiastical authority of bishops. To prevent further disorder, the privy council directed that Sunday services be suspended. Reluctantly, the king acceded to this decision. Almost before it had seen life, the prayer book had been strangled in its cradle. The episode marked a severe blow to royal and episcopal authority over the Scottish Church, and these were priorities on which the king was in the long run not inclined to compromise.

By the time that Charles was informed of its seriousness, the spark had been fanned into a conflagration. At the end of December, crowds of ministers and noblemen filled the streets of Edinburgh to present over sixty petitions to the Scottish privy council, all of them opposing the prayer book as illegally instituted and inclining towards popery. In a serious escalation, leading Scottish nobles soon joined the ministers' campaign. The cowed privy council abdicated its independent authority by forwarding the petitions to London. Every attempt Charles made to damp down the agitation only served to kindle it. His information constantly lagged behind the rapidly moving events, rendering his concessions both too little and too late. Though he had suspended use of the prayer book, the emboldened protestors now demanded a thorough reform of the Kirk, including rescinding the new canons and eliminating the Court of High Commission. In October their protest had turned violent, reducing Charles's options for compromise. He despatched north the Lord Keeper of the Scottish Privy Seal, the Earl of Roxburghe, a Scot trusted on both sides of the border, with a declaration that he intended only to advance true religion and would maintain the laws of Scotland.

But concessions regarding the liturgy were no longer enough. The ministers had whipped the populace into a frenzy and they now demanded that those bishops involved in creating the prayer book be put on trial. The more legalistic of the Supplicants, as the resisters were called at first, insisted on the summoning of a General Assembly where a programme of reform, including the repeal of the Five Articles of Perth, could be presented. Charles was now at a crossroads. Either he could take a hard line and reject their demands, or he could cave in to extortion. Almost to a man, his councillors urged the stricter course, but the king decided to compromise. In February 1638, he issued another proclamation promising that he would pardon all those who had assembled illegally in the past months and that he would give a sympathetic hearing to their petitions, but also warning that he would not tolerate any further agitation. Scottish leaders blew past this compromise formula without pause. They devised a covenant that banded them together in opposition to any religious 'innovation', a phrase that could only mean in opposition to the king's ecclesial reforms. Covenants were an important part of Scottish religious culture and this one quickly attained subscriptions, willing or forced, from most of the adult population.

Charles's efforts at appeasement had failed but he was still unwilling to accept the inevitable. He had already suspended the prayer book and, de facto, the canons. He was willing to summon a General Assembly and even a subsequent parliament, but he was not willing to accept 'the extirpation of Episcopacy'.[5] He still hoped that he could smooth over the situation. Seeking to calm the waters, he ordered his Scottish bishops to be 'sparing and moderate' in their enforcement of ceremonies.[6] In an implicit rebuke of their handling of the introduction of the prayer book, the king also ordered that General Assemblies would hence-forth determine major Church matters in his northern kingdom. Although advised by his anxious councillors to prepare for an invasion, Charles took no steps to raise forces. His chief concern was to reassert his authority, to protect episcopacy and to sunder the covenanting movement. He banked too heavily on the sheer force of majesty.

While it is patently clear that no one in England understood the depth of Scottish commitment to the covenant – 'they would rather renounce their baptism than renounce it' – it is equally clear that no one in Scotland appreciated how fundamentally Charles believed the covenant threatened his sovereignty.[7] 'I will only say that so long as this Covenant is in force ... I have no more power in Scotland than as a Duke of Venice; which I will rather die than suffer.'[8] Charles sent the Marquess of Hamilton to Edinburgh to act as royal commissioner and attempt to negotiate an end to the crisis. Hamilton was a moderate who shared the king's desire to find a peaceful solution. Yet he could find no weak spot to breach the unified Covenanter movement. He reluctantly advised that Charles prepare for war. The Covenanters, less squeamish, were making their own military preparations, seizing castles and even confiscating the crown jewels. Hamilton diagnosed the situation in political rather than religious terms: it pained him 'to see the hearts of almost every one of this kingdom alienated from their sovereign'.[9]

His advice was unwelcome. As the king reflected, the Scots were 'my own people, which by this means will be for a time ruined, so that the loss must be inevitably mine'.[10] If he wished to avoid war, he would have to make difficult concessions at the General Assembly that was summoned to meet in Glasgow in September.

The Glasgow assembly forced Charles to face reality. His northern kingdom was in rebellion and no manner of compromise could stifle it. The ministers who dominated the assembly demanded Kirk autonomy and Hamilton quickly concluded: 'there is nothing to be expected in this Assembly but madness in the highest degree'.[11] But when he attempted to dissolve the session, he was simply ignored. An entire reform programme, including the abolition of episcopacy, swept away the old Jacobean Church. The king's religious power and legislative authority were usurped. As Charles put it in his proclamation repudiating the Covenanters' actions: 'The question is ... whether we are their King or not.'[12] If war was not imminent, it was inevitable. The Scots had refused every royal offer of compromise while making none of their own. By the beginning of 1639, they were putting their nation on a war footing, summoning home from the continent Scots officers and scouring the capitals of Europe for arms and munitions. The king was finally forced to do the same. He had lost valuable time.

Neither side was committed to the impending bloodshed of the first Scottish war and negotiations opened almost immediately after the armies assembled and faced each other. The only shots fired were against an English raiding party; commanders of both armies despaired of the state of their forces. Nevertheless, there was no easy way forward. For his part, Charles abandoned his insistence that the Scots give up the covenant; the Scots, meanwhile, claimed that all they wanted was to enjoy their traditional laws and religion. But neither party meant what they said. Charles negotiated personally with the Covenanter leaders and agreed only that a new General Assembly and parliament would be summoned where the issues raised in Glasgow could be revived. This was less than the Scots wanted but more than they might obtain by force. The Pacification of Berwick, signed on 18 June, was a ceasefire rather than a treaty, and it quickly crumbled. Charles returned to London and began to make plans for a more decisive reassertion of his authority. The Scots fortified their positions and began recruiting a larger army. The clouds of war had parted for scarcely an hour before closing in again.

In retrospect, Charles's greatest chance of ending the Scottish crisis and reasserting his authority had been to fight the first Scottish war with vigour. As weak as his forces were, they were nevertheless a match for the Scots, whose logistical problems would have become insoluble. But the king had reared back from such a war on his own subjects, arguing that his actions 'not be thought to be by way of a war, but by way of a Prince, the Father of his country, his chastising his unruly children, which is never in anger, but in love and for their good'.[13] Charles hoped that the pacification would give the Scots time to rethink the wisdom of rebellion. He had consented to a General Assembly to meet at Edinburgh and then a subsequent parliament to consider the assembly's work. Both were concessions that might have led the Scots leaders to moderate their demands. However, the fact that their armies were not crushed in battle emboldened them. The Edinburgh assembly ratified all of the acts that had passed at Glasgow, including the abolition of episcopacy. After much soul-searching, the king persuaded himself that he could accept this as long as he did not need to declare episcopacy unlawful, only contrary to the constitution of the Scottish Church. This was an offer that would have saved face all around and thus one that the most aggressive Scots dismissed out of hand. Episcopacy itself had to be declared unlawful, something the king could not accept without undoing his English Church.

Compromise with the Scottish parliament was even more difficult. As the bishops were an integral part of the legislative machinery of parliament, and were the king's surest friends, their absence ensured an even more radical leadership. It was quickly clear that parliament intended to sweep aside royal authority and to become effectively sovereign. The king's hope for conciliation, never very realistic, was now shattered. He ordered his commissioner to prorogue parliament, but the members defiantly continued sitting and passing legislation without him. This act alone was a rebellion that would have been unthinkable mere months before.

Charles was now backed into the corner from which he had hoped to escape. In London his councillors were clamouring for faster preparation for war. It was clear that the contagion of resistance was spreading south. The longer the crisis lasted, the more disruptive it would become in England, where the religious cause of the Presbyterian reformers had considerable support. Effective Scottish propaganda directed at English readers converted neutrals into Scottish sympathizers. Moreover, intercepted letters strongly suggested that English Puritans were communicating with the Covenanter leaders, encouraging their resistance onwards. The Covenanters also attempted to secure aid from the King of France, treason that should have heightened anti-Scottish sentiment in London. The Privy Council advised Charles to summon Parliament, the prescribed remedy for repelling a military threat and his first in eleven years. While the king and his advisers anticipated a rocky session, they did not anticipate that a parliament would refuse an English king when 'his kingdoms and person are in apparent danger'.[14] An army was camped at the northern border poised to invade. It was Parliament's responsibility to supply the king.

The most interesting question about the three-week Short Parliament is not why it was so short, but why it was so long. It lasted only from 13 April to 5 May 1640 and, from the start, parliamentary leaders made clear their intention to block war supply. Some had colluded with the Scots and could now hardly allow Parliament to finance a war against them. Their chief tactic was to stall. The king appealed for haste; the Commons responded with delay. John Pym, a Commons leader from the 1620s, produced a list of thirty-six separate grievances and called for the creation of three time-consuming committees to examine them. The session began with attacks upon the king's prerogative revenues, including those from impositions and ship money. Records from the court cases on those levies were acquired and committees began the tedious process of re-examining the judges' decisions. After personally opening the parliament, Charles reappeared only a week later to hasten progress on supply. The Commons spent an entire day debating whether to take his desperate appeal into consideration. After another week, he reappeared to promise on the word of a king that he would redress their grievances if they would pledge funding. The members would not trust the king's pledge. Finally, when a royal councillor suggested that Charles would repudiate ship money in return for twelve subsidies, the lawyers tied him in knots by arguing that if the levy were illegal then Parliament should not purchase its surrender, and if it were legal, then the king could not renounce it for any price. Charles offered every possible compromise and each was rebuffed. Everything was done to provoke the king – even the pretence of blaming evil councillors for the king's malefactions was abandoned – until finally his patience snapped. His army was assembling and he intended to join it.

Though the king did not secure parliamentary funding for the second Scottish war, he was not without resources. The Irish parliament had granted subsidies, loans were secured from his privy councillors and military levies were the responsibility of the counties. His combined forces probably totalled twenty thousand men, but the inadequacy of his army was quickly exposed. His summons of the Yorkshire militia resulted in local debate about whether the forces could be removed from the county. Charles's three-pronged strategy of invading from Ireland, the west of Scotland and the north of England collapsed, leaving his army in a weak

and vulnerable position. Moreover, the Scots better understood their own military situation. If they didn't attack first
and invade England, they would not be able to feed their
forces. As so often in early modern Europe, the need to provision an army encouraged aggression. Thus at the end of
August 1640, the Covenanters crossed the Tweed and in
one decisive battle defeated English forces and stormed and
captured the fortified town of Newcastle. The Scots now
controlled the London coal supply and had an unobstructed
path to York, England's second city. As he twisted to survey
this disaster, Charles might have felt the noose tightening.

5
Reform and Rebellion

The implications of the Scottish invasion sunk in slowly. Initially Charles believed that he could reinvigorate his forces and revive his cause. All he needed was money. The king summoned the nobility to a great council of peers at York. Surely they would not abandon a sovereign in distress? But such optimism quickly faded. Even his most aggressive councillors realized there was little hope of preventing further Scottish incursions and no hope of military resurgence. The Scots were ensconced in well-fortified positions and living off the fatted farms of Durham and Northumberland. They would not be easily dislodged.

By the time the peers arrived in the north, Charles had already decided that his only option was to summon another parliament and attempt to negotiate a ceasefire until it could meet. Because the Scots refused to treat with the king, he sent the Earl of Bristol to propose the mutual disbandment of the armies. The Scots replied that they would only present their terms to the English parliament. In the meantime, Charles could either pay for the maintenance of their forces or accept the spoliation of the counties they controlled. Incapable of funding one army, the king was now burdened with supporting two.

Charles I's confidence had been shaken by the events of mid 1640. First his English subjects had refused his pleas for military support, then the Scottish rebels had won a rapid and unexpected victory over his armies. His advisers no longer presented alternatives. He would have to face a parliament that would be intent on stripping him of his prerogatives and restricting his powers. Even those who, like Strafford, understood that they were likely to be targets of parliamentary investigation and punishment, advised Charles to swallow whatever pride remained and acquiesce to their terms.

The Long Parliament, which sat for thirteen years, assembled on 4 November 1640 amid a mood of jubilation in London. The accumulated grievances of the past decade now counterbalanced the peace and prosperity that the king had achieved. They ran in familiar parliamentary channels: attacks on the king's ministers; complaints of extra-parliamentary taxation, such as ship money and impositions; and, most passionately, repudiation of real and perceived religious innovations. The leadership of the Long Parliament was in a very strong position. They had the leverage of the Scottish army to create urgency for reform, they could draw on a palpable anger shared by most members against an array of royal policies, and they had the zeal of the numerous Puritans among them. They also enjoyed widespread support out of doors. At Westminster, crowds assembled in the Palace Yard while petitions for reform flooded in from the counties, many of them carefully co-ordinated by zealous ministers. Nevertheless, their position of strength had one glaring weakness. A number of

MPs had actively committed treason by conspiring with the Scots. They could not come to any settlement with Charles that did not somehow include amnesty for their treachery. Since their encouragement of the Scots was based on the belief that Charles could not be trusted, how could they now trust him with their lives?

The parliamentary leadership worked to solve this problem methodically, first by stripping Charles of his ablest ministers. Within days the Earl of Strafford was in the Tower and within weeks Archbishop Laud and Bishop Matthew Wren were similarly imprisoned. The MPs opened inquiries against Lord Chancellor Finch, who had issued the ship money judgement, and Secretary Windebank, who was responsible for the king's correspondence. Both fled to the continent. Assuming a legal function it had never before possessed, the House of Commons also examined the judges who had ruled against Hampden. Next, having isolated the king from his advisers, the members worked to limit his powers. Already, in the Short Parliament, the king's prerogative to summon and dissolve parliaments had been challenged. Now the parliamentary leaders sought to abolish it. A triennial act was prepared, mandating that a new session be summoned once every three years. It was presented for Charles's signature simultaneously with a subsidy bill to pay the armies. He could not have one without the other. In order to preserve their legislative reforms, the parliamentary leadership made it impossible for the king to dissolve Parliament. A bill empowered only the Long Parliament to dissolve itself, thereby ensuring that it would sit for the remainder of Charles's life. Meanwhile, the

Commons began a systematic campaign to strip away royal revenues, abolishing ship money, impositions and royal grants of patents and monopolies. The king was now so impoverished that Parliament found it necessary to vote him an allowance.

Charles was bowed but not yet broken. Publicly he acquiesced to parliamentary reform while privately seeking an opportunity to draw the line. At this stage he had only a handful of powerless supporters in the Commons. Reform was on everyone's lips. Committees were appointed to abolish the prerogative courts of Star Chamber and High Commission and the regional judiciaries of the Council of the North and of the Marches of Wales. Even the Court of Admiralty came under attack. The lawyers who dominated the Lower House of Parliament were intent on eliminating every judiciary that did not adhere to the common law.

However, two obstacles blocked the unimpeded triumph of parliamentary reform. First, there was no agreement on religion. Book licensing, which sanctioned publication, collapsed with Star Chamber and High Commission unleashing a torrent of print, some of it avowedly separatist and much of it shockingly radical. The Presbyterians, once extreme Puritans, were now driven to the centre as splinter groups formed, advocating various congregational polities. For the moment, religious reformers could at least rally around the abolition of episcopacy, but they wished it for different ends. In any case, there was a considerable faction of MPs who sought at most a moderated episcopacy, and rejected its abolition. Secondly, despite the fact that they had colluded with the Scots, the leaders of the Long

Parliament found it no easier to negotiate with them than had the king. The Scots insisted upon the establishment of Scottish-style Presbyterianism in England as the only reliable security for their Kirk in Scotland. They also pressed for a punitive settlement of their political differences with the king, stripping him of most attributes of sovereignty and punishing all those who had supported him. The Scots showed no inclination towards compromise despite the fact that their settlement would have to be approved by the king. Charles had already rejected the notion that his loyal Scottish councillors would be handed over for treason trials.

At the end of January 1641, Charles summoned the Members of Parliament to plead for an end to the crisis. He reminded them of the mounting bill to pay the two armies; indeed, the Scots had just submitted a demand for an additional £500,000, shocking the parliamentary commissioners. In a spirit of reconciliation, the king pledged to end innovations in religion, to abolish burdensome taxes and to revamp the judicial system – that is, to accept the core of the reforms being voted in the Commons. Shortly thereafter, he appointed seven prominent parliamentary leaders to the Privy Council. But he stood firm against attacks on his crown, his Church and his councillors. He refused to allow the usurpation of his right to convoke parliaments. He also opposed the removal of the bishops from the House of Lords, and the execution of his loyal servants.

If Charles had lost his vigour, he had kept to his principles. These would be tested shortly. No less than the king, who believed that a few fiery spirits orchestrated opposition to him, the parliamentary leaders believed that a few evil councillors were the cause of the kingdom's ills. The chief of these, once a darling of the House of Commons, was the Earl of Strafford, who had brought order to Ireland. His active role in English government was only recent, but he was an ardent supporter of the Scottish war. It was feared that Strafford possessed evidence demonstrating the treason of the parliamentary leaders. As a result, he was excluded from the House of Lords and imprisoned. His impeachment dominated events in the spring. The case, spearheaded by Pym, rested on three elements: Strafford's violation of Irish law as Lord Deputy; his advice that the king make war against the Scots by any means necessary; and his recommendation that an Irish army be brought into England to subdue opposition. Only the third set of charges could be stretched to fall under the rubrics of the treason statute and it could only be demonstrated by perjured testimony and evidentiary legerdemain. However, the Scots were goading parliamentary leaders who feared Strafford more than they feared the king: 'the great remora to all matters is the head of Strafford'.[1]

Charles once promised Strafford that he would not allow him to suffer 'in life, honour, or fortune' for his loyal service, but he found himself powerless to intervene in the proceedings.[2] Strafford needed little assistance. Weak in body but strong in spirit, he brilliantly parried the flimsy charges against him. The seething animosity of his accusers could not overcome the legal inadequacy of their case. They had to abandon the impeachment. Instead, they determined

1. This portrait of Charles as Duke of York was
commissioned by Cambridge University in 1613.

2. Charles I and Henrietta Maria, 1632: the queen presents
her husband with a laurel crown to symbolize their union. This
is a copy of Van Dyck's original, which in itself was a copy of an
inferior painting by Mytens.

3. One of the many sumptuous paintings of Charles
and his family by Van Dyck, c.1632

4. Charles in armour riding through a triumphal arch, painted by Van Dyck, 1633. Carrying a military baton and adorned with the ribbon of the Order of the Garter, he is accompanied by his riding master, Pierre Antoine Bourdon, Seigneur de St Antoine.

5. This triple portrait was painted by Van Dyck in 1635 so that the great Italian sculptor Bernini could model a bust of Charles. Notice the prominence of his lovelock, the long hair on his left side.

6. William Laud, Archbishop of Canterbury, was a patron of scholarship at Oxford University. Portrait by Van Dyck, *c.*1635–7.

7. Thomas Wentworth, shown with a mastiff. This was painted while he was Lord Deputy of Ireland. Portrait by Van Dyck, *c.*1633–6.

8. Van Dyck's *Charles I on Horseback*, *c*.1637–8, depicts the king in full armour but in a pastoral setting. He is placed on a great horse to disguise his slight stature.

9. Charles at his trial, painted by Edward Bower, 1648. His hair and beard are untended as he was not allowed a barber during his captivity.

to proceed by bill of attainder, an act of Parliament that simply declared the earl guilty. To take effect the attainder had to pass the Lords and receive the assent of the king. Rioting mobs appeared outside the House of Lords screaming for blood and threatening vengeance. Wild rumours of an attempted coup to rescue Strafford easily cowed the attenuated Upper House. Next it was the king's conscience that had to be sacrificed. Charles, fearing for the safety of his family, consulted his spiritual advisers about breaking his promise, but Strafford had already absolved him. Under intense pressure from his councillors, the king gave his unwilling consent. Strafford was executed on 11 May.

For the next several months, Charles retreated inside himself. He instantly regretted his capitulation – it would haunt him for the rest of his life – and now thought of himself as weak and vulnerable. He acquiesced without resistance to the bills that stripped his prerogatives. Parliament gained control of its own dissolution, the judiciary was reorganized and new taxes were imposed, all consented to by a dazed monarch, 'he having granted all hitherto demanded by Parliament'.[3] The continual crisis wearied him and there was no end in sight. More ominously, there was still no progress over a treaty with the Scots. Pym, now fearful that he could no longer hold his coalition together, made an initial attempt at a settlement with the king that included a general pardon that would excuse past treason. But the stipulations that Parliament would choose the king's councillors and the queen's household were more than even a chastened Charles would swallow. Slowly he awoke from his slumber and decided to take matters into his own hands. The Scottish crisis had to be resolved and Charles determined to settle it by going to Edinburgh. With one bold move he would reassert his authority.

To settle with the Scots, Charles surrendered everything for which he had fought. He agreed to accept the acts passed by the renegade Edinburgh parliament, consented to the abolition of episcopacy and placed in positions of power all of his inveterate enemies. In return, the Scottish army withdrew from England. The Scottish wars were over. Now, stripped of his prerogatives and most of his authority, Charles was received in regal splendour by the Scots. On his return south, he was met with cheering crowds along the highways and found his path paved with flowers.

Such fair skies for the king boded ill for the parliamentary leaders. Their agenda remained unfinished. At its head was religion. The Lords had already rejected a bill to exclude the bishops from their House. Agitation to abolish episcopacy 'root and branch' continued unabated and temporary religious unity was achieved only by waves of anti-Catholic agitation. Sketchy details of plots to rescue Strafford were intertwined with tales of papist conspiracies. Ten Propositions submitted by Parliament before Charles's trip to Scotland were laced with anti-Catholic clauses. Attacks upon the queen and her Catholic advisers were ratcheted up. Anti-popery came in waves and at the end of 1641 one of them was cresting.

It became a tsunami with news of rebellion in Ireland. A violent rising of Catholics against Protestants left thousands dead, primarily in Ulster, where Protestant depredations against the native population had been most intense. The old English threw in their lot with the Gaelic Irish, hoping to achieve the same level of concessions as had the Scots. The reality of the rising was grisly enough, but lurid and exaggerated accounts – fully illustrated in printed woodcuts – were met by a visceral rage in Parliament. To suppress it, money was raised by subscription on the security of Irish land that would be confiscated. As matters stood, however, military power remained in the hands of the king. Few in Parliament were willing to trust Charles with an army, especially after the fabricated evidence against Strafford suggested that he would use that army in England. The parliamentary leaders were now hoist by their own petards.

Under all of these pressures, the leaders of the Long Parliament chose to put forward a Grand Remonstrance that summarized their lengthy list of grievances against the king. Their motives will always be a matter of speculation. Were they angered by the king's policies? Were they jealous of Charles's success in Scotland? Did they fear that the king might move to suppress them by force? In any case, the debates over the Grand Remonstrance broke apart the parliamentary reform movement. Many members wanted no part in publicizing their grievances, 'to tell stories to the people and talk of the king as of a third person'.[4]

Charles had regained some of his old confidence by the time that he received the remonstrance along with a petition demanding that Parliament choose the monarch's councillors. He sensed that his subjects wished an end to the unrelenting crises gripping England and now spilling over into Ireland. He had already consented to massive reforms of his government, sacrificed his loyal ministers and revoked his own prerogatives. Parliamentary leaders would not cease stripping his powers until he was king in name only. Well might he ponder: 'I do not ask what you have done for me.'[5] The answer was plain.

Charles decided to put an end to the forced erosion of his monarchical powers by having five leading members of the Commons arrested on the long-deferred treason charges. Unfortunately, news of his plans leaked and the targeted members fled Westminster while legal papers were being drawn up. As a result, the king's extraordinary entrance into a sitting House of Commons on 4 January 1642 had the opposite effect to the one intended. The Speaker refused to answer his monarch's direct enquiry and, as the king retreated, the members shouted 'privilege, privilege'. Charles had gambled and lost. A divided Commons so threatened was again united. The accused parliamentary leaders returned in triumph and the era of co-operation between king and Parliament was at an end.

Shortly thereafter, Charles and his family left London, a practical necessity with pressure mounting to impeach the queen, but a tactical calamity. Parliament now controlled the City's stores of arms and treasure, its well-trained militia and most of the king's navy. The constitutional difficulties that Parliament might have faced with the king in London arguing for peace evaporated overnight. The notion was born that the consent of any two parts of the legislature was greater than the dissent of the other. This effectively deposed Charles. The lawyers engaged in some tortured finessing of precedent in order to create a new class of legislation known as ordinances that would have the force of law without the consent of the king. The most important of these gave Parliament power to raise and command troops and levy taxes for their support. The Earl of Essex was appointed parliamentary Lord General and put in charge of an army formed from the London trained bands.

If Parliament controlled material resources, the king marshalled emotional ones. The culture of loyalty to the monarch was deeply engrained in England. Over time this would prove Charles's greatest asset, one that could not be destroyed on a battlefield. His first concern was to secure the safety of Henrietta Maria, who departed for the Netherlands in the spring. He knew he was incapable of resisting any extortion demanded with his wife as hostage. He also was aware that he needed to play for time while building a military machine. As distasteful as it was, he would have to deal with an implacable parliamentary leadership. In February 1642, he acquiesced to the exclusion of the bishops from the Lords. But in March, when it was demanded that he voluntarily cede his military powers, Charles snapped. 'You have asked that of me in this was never asked of any king and with which I will not trust my wife and children.'[6] Moreover, by now the parliamentary cause had been sundered. Nearly half of those originally selected to the Long Parliament took the king's side, as did most of the peers. When Parliament presented its Nineteen Propositions in June, they were summarily rejected. These were terms for unconditional surrender, as even the king's most moderate advisers opined. The king would not give over his right to consent to legislation, control of his military, his choice of officers or supervision of his children. Nor would he grant a pardon to those who had committed treason. He had decided, as he wrote some months later to the Marquess of Hamilton, to 'be either a glorious king or a patient martyr'.[7] The king's *Answer to the Nineteen Propositions* was published and became the first Royalist propaganda success of the war. It convincingly portrayed the Parliamentarians as destroyers of the traditional constitutional balance and usurpers of royal powers. The excesses of Parliament had created a party for the king.

In the summer of 1642, Charles began raising troops to wage war against Parliament. He borrowed money from the peerage, many of whom were motivated by news that Parliament planned to confiscate the estates of royal supporters. The king's presence was an incomparable advantage and his forces swelled whenever he appeared. Though Charles had a nominal command structure, he served as his own general, sitting at the head of the council of war. He soon recruited battle-hardened generals, including Sir Jacob Astley, who had first fought alongside Sir Walter Raleigh, and his royal nephews Princes Rupert and Maurice, who had engaged in Germany to restore their parents' patrimony. Like Parliament, he appointed peers to serve as his regional generals and, given the state of communications, granted them considerable autonomy. At the end of August 1642, his standard was hoisted at Nottingham. It bore the motto 'Give Caesar His Due'.

Though it took months to begin, the war opened ferociously. Charles's strategic objective was plain: to recapture London. After recruiting in the north, the royal army, numbering over fourteen thousand, turned south and met the parliamentary forces at Edgehill. Royalist cavalry under Rupert overpowered their opponents, though the infantry did not fare as well. By the end of the battle the king's forces were on the offensive and had an open path to the capital. At the council of war Charles's advisers struck a cautious note, but the king insisted on making a dash to London and ending the war with one blow. The strategy came very close to succeeding. Rupert's troops crossed the Thames at Brentford, put its garrison to the sword and were allowed to plunder. This was an omen not lost on the governors of London, who pressured Parliament to treat for peace. Nevertheless, the sack of Brentford had two less desirable consequences. It gave the Earl of Essex time to reassemble his forces and arrive in London; it also stimulated a tenacious defence of their city by ordinary people who feared encountering Rupert's rampaging men. When the two armies faced each other at Turnham Green in November, parliamentary forces, though less experienced, were double those of the king's. Considering discretion to be the better part of valour, Charles retired into winter quarters at Oxford, which was to become his capital throughout the war. It may have been his best chance at victory.

For the next three years, the civil war played to a single rhythm: fighting from spring to autumn followed by fruitless peace negotiations during the winter. Hardliners battled for their own preservation, as both king and Parliament had declared their opponents traitors, while moderates tried to broker a settlement. The various sets of proposals presented to the king were not much improvement on the Nineteen Propositions, for Parliament deemed all the key issues to be non-negotiable. As the Royalist Earl of Clarendon observed, the Oxford Proposals of 1643 'were so unreasonable, that they well knew that the king would never consent to them'.[8] Both sides dug in for another campaign and neither achieved much advantage. The Royalists took Bristol but not Gloucester and the Battle of Newbury ended in stalemate. The queen returned to England, bringing arms, ammunition and her adamantine resolve. The reunion did much to buoy Charles's spirits. It was the last time he would see her.

The English civil war turned British just before the campaign of 1644. Parliament negotiated a covenant with the Scots that brought their army into England once again, while Charles arranged a cessation with the Irish Catholics that freed his Protestant troops there to arrive in the west. Both sides believed their alliances gave them the decisive advantage. Events proved each of them wrong. The involvement of all three British kingdoms in the war merely served to prolong and envenom it. A spectacular Royalist victory at Cropredy Bridge, where Charles's presence inspired his troops, was followed by the loss of the north when the Scottish army contributed to royal defeats at Marston Moor and York. Though it looked as if the Parliamentarians had finally made the long-sought military breakthrough after these northern battles, a series of tactical errors led them to snatch defeat from the jaws of victory. The Earl of Essex managed to trap his own infantry in Cornwall where the king surrounded it and forced surrender. There was no massacre of the defeated. The soldiers simply laid down their arms and marched away. They shortly re-formed and faced the king a second time at Newbury where Charles retrieved his captured artillery. Another year's fighting had resulted in another year of deadlock.

By now the war had taken on its own momentum and moderates on both sides were desperate to find an accommodation. In Parliament, recriminations among commanders led to the 'new modelling' of their forces and the elimination of traditional aristocratic commanders. Never were those inclined to peace in a stronger position in the Lower House, yet the proposals sent to the king at Uxbridge were more stringent than those he had rejected the year before. The war's stalemate made concessions ever more necessary, but its enormous toll of blood and expended treasure made them more psychologically difficult. Extremists on both sides continued to fear that they would be sacrificed as part of any bargain. Private conversations between the king and the parliamentary commissioners demonstrated the depth of divisions at Westminster and revealed that there was no possibility that the sides could strike a deal on even the most moderate terms that would be acceptable to Parliament. As Charles wrote to his wife, 'this summer will be the hottest for war of any that hath been yet'.[9]

Up to this point, strategic wisdom had dictated that forces be divided so that no single encounter was decisive. In the spring of 1645, all this changed. Parliament's purpose in remodelling its forces was to create a streamlined and proactive military that would aggressively pursue the king. The king's military leaders, on the other hand, wrongly believed that this new parliamentary army was weak and disorganized. Both were willing to risk a potentially decisive showdown. It took place on 14 June at Naseby. Charles's forces were outnumbered, but it was thought they would be better co-ordinated and their cavalry more experienced. As it transpired, Rupert was unable to restrain his marauding troops in the heat of battle while his counterpart, Oliver Cromwell, was able to control his. The Parliamentarians secured an incontestable victory. Over a thousand Royalists were slain and nearly five thousand captured, along with the king's artillery and his private correspondence with his wife. If Naseby did not end the English civil war, it made it impossible for Charles to win it. But ultimate victory also eluded Parliament. At this point, the king was the lone participant in the war whom no side could label a traitor. His greatest asset, even in defeat, remained his legitimacy. Stripping him of that would elevate civil war into revolution.

6

Revolution and Regicide

Throughout the war, the king had shown courage and determination. He stalked the camps and shared the experiences of his men. Mornings were spent reading despatches and news from London, all of which was brought to him daily in thick bundles. He then walked in the Oxford gardens where he consulted with his advisers and received petitions. During his ordeal he was an active and conscientious monarch. Moreover, he was present at his army's battles. At Naseby, as his troops were slaughtered, he attempted to charge on to the battlefield, only to be pulled away by a loyal retainer. Now was not the time for empty gestures of sacrifice, Charles was told.

On his retreat westward, the king tried to put a brave face on the military calamity, though he knew in his heart that the war was lost. Anticipating his capture, he sent secret instructions to his son not to yield to parliamentary extortion. He also implored Clarendon to ensure that his heir was taken safely out of the kingdom. Fruitless attempts to garner reinforcements from Ireland and the continent continued apace. The publication of his letters to his wife proved a propaganda disaster. They contained the damaging offer to suspend the penal laws against Catholics if any Catholic power would assist him. James had offered similar concessions to both Spain and France during his son's marriage negotiations, but in the superheated atmosphere of the civil war, Charles's offer was interpreted as the first step towards reconverting England to popery. By now Parliament, with most religious traditionalists fled to the king, had dismantled the old episcopal Church. In January of 1645, Archbishop Laud had followed Strafford to the scaffold. A hysterical fear of popery had fuelled most of this religious revolution.

The autumn fighting was intense. At Naseby, Parliamentarians had executed a hundred Welsh women camp followers on the mistaken assumption that they were Irish. This stiffened the resolve in the fortified Royalist strongholds throughout the West Country. The sieges of Taunton, Bridgwater and Bath were strenuous. The Battle of Langport was hard fought before the New Model Army made its breakthrough. Bristol and Chester were both lost and Charles's hopes in Scotland were dashed at Philiphaugh, with the defeat and brutal execution of the Highlanders who had followed the Marquess of Montrose. Though the king had spent these months attempting to rally his troops, he experienced one defeat after another. As he went into winter quarters at the beginning of 1646, his thoughts turned towards settlement.

If Charles was never willing to capitulate to his opponents, he had shown himself more flexible than the Parliamentarians, who essentially demanded his military surrender and constitutional emasculation. He took betrayal seriously because he believed loyalty was the glue that bound together a monarchy. When men, such as the duplicitous Earl of Northumberland, whom he had advanced, turned against him, he could not muster any trace of forgiveness. This was especially true of the Scottish nobility, many of whom he had made rich and very few of whom stood with him in the testing hour.

Charles pondered revenge while contemplating peace. Both before and after Naseby, overtures were made in both directions. He would have sacrificed much to win a military victory, and no doubt his leading enemies would have paid a price for their treachery. Yet there is little reason to believe that he would have exacted as great a revenge as was demanded by Parliament against his loyal supporters. While dreams of a military reversal of fortune fed his fantasies, finding acceptable terms for peace dominated his reality. After Naseby, old friends privately made tentative suggestions for possible grounds of accord, but all such schemes faltered on the unwillingness of the Parliamentarians to make even token gestures of reconciliation. Attitudes had hardened in Westminster as the blood and treasure continued to flow. It was expected that the king, having surrendered on the field of military combat, would likewise yield in the political fray. He was not inclined to abandon his remaining advantage: his royal prestige. Thus there was not the slightest inclination towards compromise, whatever the king suggested.

It is commonplace to regard Charles as desperate after the defeat of his armies. In truth, he never thought that government could be recomposed without him. Thus when it was clear that he could not find agreement with Parliament, he considered alternatives. For a few weeks in 1646, he contemplated fleeing to the continent and personally appealing to its crowned heads for aid. Then he thought of arriving in London and appealing to the people to restore his reformed government. Ultimately, he decided to flee to the Scots in an effort to divide them from their English allies. Having already granted the Scots religious autonomy and constitutional protection, he imagined that the price of a new alliance might be far less than what the Parliamentarians were demanding.

The Scots and the English had fallen out over a range of issues, not the least of which was the form Presbyterianism was to take in England. In 1646, Parliament had voted the establishment of a Presbyterian Church firmly under civil control – 'a lame Erastian Presbytery,' as one of the Scots commissioners complained.[1] Even that watered-down Church settlement attracted criticism from Parliament's non-Presbyterian supporters. The gathered Churches were as opposed to a Protestant state religion as they were to Catholicism. 'New *Presbyter* is but old *Priest* writ large' was John Milton's piercing observation.[2]

Allying with the Scots promised to give Charles leverage in two different ways. Their army might resuscitate his military fortunes, or the mere threat of renewed war might force Parliament to soften its demands. In order to begin negotiations, Charles appeared suddenly and unexpectedly in the Scottish camp at Newark, disguised as a servant. Having effectively surrendered to the Scots, he was taken to Newcastle to await the arrival of parliamentary commissioners.

Charles's hopes did not bear fruit immediately. Having insisted on the formulation of joint terms of peace, the Scots could not now enter into separate negotiations with the king. Privately they insisted that Charles convert to Presbyterianism. In July 1646, the commissioners arrived at Newcastle with a new set of propositions. They contained the familiar, non-negotiable demands: the abolition of episcopacy, the abdication of military power for twenty years, parliamentary control over future royal appointments and strict measures against Catholics. There were clauses protecting Scottish special interests as well as those of the city of London. But by far the longest part of the proposals involved the retribution that Parliament and the Scots intended to exact. Dozens of leading Royalists were fully exempted from pardon and would be subject to treason prosecutions and execution. Dozens of others were to have a third of their estates confiscated and would be banned from court. Thousands were disabled from holding offices in the localities. There was to be no gesture towards reconciliation. Royalists were to pay for the war in every possible way. To concede these terms would have required an act of rank royal betrayal. Given Charles's character, it was an unimaginable step.

Charles made several serious gestures towards peace while at Newcastle. He ordered the Highland Royalists to disband their forces and he sent Montrose into exile. He agreed to be instructed in Presbyterianism by the great Scottish divine Alexander Henderson, and the two conducted a seven-week theological disputation that would have confirmed James's opinion that his son could hold his own in any religious controversy. The king also offered to suppress radical Puritanism, Independency, which wished for a congregational rather than a national Church, and sectarianism, which wished for no established Church at all, and allow for the introduction of Presbyterianism into parts of England provided he could retain Anglican bishops elsewhere.

Critics believed that these offers were insincere and that Charles was playing for time as relations between Parliament and Scots worsened. Furthermore, he still had hopes of reinforcements from France or Ireland, which also required time. That the king was keeping all options open is certain, but this does not mean that he did not honestly seek a negotiated settlement. The proposals he sent were no more intransigent than the ones he received but viewed charitably might have been regarded as opening gambits in a process of negotiation. He was besieged on all sides by demands that he abandon the episcopal Church and it took considerable courage to refuse not only his enemies but also his wife and his supporters, many of whom disliked his pious conscientiousness. It will never be known if Parliament would have diluted the rest of its demands had Charles given way over religion. They had not shown any inclination towards compromise and the private overtures presented to him in these months had not emanated from Westminster. The Scots, meanwhile, were just as stiff-necked as the English. After being 'barbarously treated', the king now was given an ultimatum: renounce his religion or be returned into the hands of Parliament.[3] He refused. At the end of December, the Scots again removed their army from

English soil, having ransomed their monarch for £400,000, only half of which they ever received.

For the next three months, the king's existence depended upon the whim of his captors. Troops guarded him and parliamentary commissioners attended him. He was interned at Holmby House in Northamptonshire, where he was denied access to his servants and his chaplains. One of his predictions, however, had come true. The Parliamentarians had not been able to end the crises without him. The Presbyterian majority in the Commons embarked upon a plan to settle the main issues in contention and present the king with a fait accompli. They ordered the sale of bishops' estates, thereby hoping to solidify the new Presbyterian Church; they organized an expeditionary force to exact revenge upon the Irish Catholics; and made plans to disband the bulk of the army. All the while the king awaited his fate. He continued to propose concessions for a settlement, agreeing to accept Presbyterianism for a three-year period and to relinquish control of the militia for a decade. He was clearly garnering support, though opposition to his demand that he be allowed to come to London unified his opponents. Smuggled letters recounted the same hollow tales of imminent foreign aid and elaborate schemes to effect his escape, but there is little evidence to suggest that Charles was an active participant in any of these Royalist pipe dreams.

Nor did the king anticipate the military coup that was to prove so consequential in determining his ultimate fate. On the evening of 3 June 1647, a contingent of New Model troops arrived at Holmby and ordered the king to accompany them to army headquarters. He had no means to resist, but it is an error to believe that he immediately saw this as an opportunity. In fact he was terrified that the soldiers intended to assassinate him – 'he was very apprehensive in what hands he was' – and insisted that the parliamentary commissioners attend them as witnesses.[4]

The army's intervention in politics transformed the conclusion of the civil war into the beginning of the revolution. Disgusted by their captious treatment by Parliament, the junior officers and rank and file took matters into their own hands and their leaders, especially Oliver Cromwell and Henry Ireton, could only race to catch up. Both were members of the House of Commons and thus in a position to broker an accommodation between army, king and Parliament. Moreover, the army's intervention annihilated the Scottish alliance. All along, the Scots had insisted upon an English Presbyterian establishment as a bulwark for the safety of their own Kirk. With the army purged of its Presbyterian officers and in possession of the king, the Scots had lost their leverage. They now appealed, with serpentine calculation, to the once abandoned Charles. At the same time, not entirely sure of their dominance, the army leaders presented their own overtures to the king. Sitting at the balance of power, Charles now received markedly better treatment. He was allowed Anglican services, had loyal attendants restored and was given freedom to converse and communicate. He managed to persuade his captors to incarcerate him in Windsor Castle, a fully functional royal palace. When the army's propositions for constitutional settlement known as the Heads of Proposals were presented to him, he was favourably inclined to many of their conditions. He was willing to tolerate Independency if the Independents were willing to tolerate him. Again he asked that episcopacy be explicitly permitted. The sectarians of the army proved more reasonable than the Presbyterians on the ultimately crucial question of religion.

There can be no doubt that the Heads of Proposals were the best terms that Charles was ever offered. Their rejection was a lost opportunity. Where Parliament sent him non-negotiable demands, the army was willing to seek adjustments if the main principles were accepted. Their terms were also more congenial. Only seven of Charles's loyal supporters would be exempted from pardon; after a brief hiatus, former Royalists could re-enter government; the king would share power with a council of state that would gradually relinquish it back to the crown. It was a handsome offer if those who made it were sincere and had the power to bring it about. This was the king's dilemma. As much as he despised his parliamentary opponents, he understood the source of their authority. He could be confident that an agreement with Parliament would have the force of law. But what was an army and what authority did it have to impose a political settlement?

Charles was deeply distrustful of Cromwell and Ireton, with whom his principal advisers negotiated. Since the junior officers and rank and file had set up a parallel organization, Charles shrewdly perceived that its commanders were not actually leading the army. Charles was also concerned that any concessions made to the army would also have to be made to the Parliament if the Heads of Proposals were rejected. He asked the army leaders point blank whether they could assure parliamentary compliance with their proposals. He received only vague assurances. Moreover, his negotiations with the Independents in the army terrified the Scottish and parliamentary Presbyterians. The Scots, who had rejected a military option when Charles threw himself upon their mercy, were now eager to conclude an agreement that would back the king with force. Given the fact that these groups kept offering to sweeten the pot in return for royal support, Charles might be forgiven for thinking that he could play them all off against each other and emerge with his authority intact.

But events were to prove this impossible. The army's initial purge of the Presbyterian leadership in the Commons split the parliamentary movement. The army's influence increased further when it marched into London to restore order in the two Houses. With the army's backing, the Independents now shared power at Westminster, but they failed to persuade their colleagues to soften the terms for peace. The king offered another olive branch, promising to further water down episcopal authority, agreeing to the establishment of Presbyterianism for three years, and (most remarkably) abdicating military authority during his lifetime. Parliament, however, responded with the Four Bills, comprising the same non-negotiable conditions that had been proposed at Newcastle.

At this point, Charles became a victim of his own rising popularity. The majority of the nation wanted the king restored at almost any price. Pamphleteers, meanwhile, demanded that he be brought to London to negotiate a personal treaty. A creeping sense of isolation hardened attitudes among those who had fought against him. A bungled attempt at royal escape led to his removal from the comforts of Windsor to the rigours of Carisbrooke Castle near Newport on the Isle of Wight.

Charles was now faced with two unpalatable choices: close with the Scots and attempt a military solution or surrender to Parliament and rule as a figurehead. It is wrong to regard Charles as either insincere or untrustworthy in his dealings with the army and the Scots. To the one he was willing to tolerate Independency, and to the other he was willing to suppress it. To him, one heresy was the same as another. But in neither case was he willing to surrender the demand that he be allowed to practise his own faith and govern the English Church as its supreme head. On Christmas Day 1647, he chose to side with the Scots.

The war that ensued surpassed in ferocity anything that had been known on English soil. Confronted by a Royalist rising, the New Model Army recomposed itself into a disciplined fighting force. Regiments besieged strongholds in Wales and Yorkshire, while a detachment led by Sir Thomas Fairfax encircled Colchester. Meanwhile, the Scottish army, on which the king had pinned his hopes, made its disorderly entrance into England. Its commander, the Marquess of Hamilton, faced internal divisions that deprived him of the veteran soldiers needed to stand up to seasoned New Model troops. The Battle of Preston in August 1648 was a rout. Cromwell drove the Scots from the field while his soldiers pursued them relentlessly for nearly a week. The Scots surrendered in their thousands despite their greater number.

News of this result ended the Royalist holdout in Colchester. The garrison surrendered on mercy and two of its commanders were executed by firing squad. The gentleman's war between king and Parliament had turned truly vicious. While rash soldiers had once whispered of the deposition of the king, Charles was now openly referred to as 'that man of blood' in army councils. This second civil war erased the mounting sympathy for a royal restoration. In the army there was talk of a trial; in Parliament, discussions focused on a final round of peace proposals, but no one now trusted the king.

It is difficult to know what Charles had expected from his alliance with the Scots. The initial Royalist risings throughout England had demonstrated that he still had deep support among his subjects, but whether that was due to love of the king or fear of the army was impossible to gauge. Many English Presbyterians, alarmed by rising sectarianism and the assertiveness of the army, began to repent of their role in the first war and lent moral and material backing to the king in the second. But the outcome of the second civil war imperilled the king. What had been a world of possibilities in the winter shrank considerably by summer. He would either have to close with the parliamentary commissioners, who arrived carrying yet another version of the unpalatable Newcastle Propositions, or accept the possibility that he would be deposed or worse. At Carisbrooke Castle he was far away from the centre of events, but his captors allowed him free access to news, correspondence and visitors. He knew that the political temperature was rising against him.

He had finally decided to capitulate. There was to be no negotiation at Newport. He was required openly to take responsibility for the war and to accept the full abandonment of military power, the abolition of the episcopal Church and liquidation of much of its wealth, and parliamentary control of court appointments. Each night, as a testament for his son and heir, he recorded in detail what he had accepted and what reservations he had offered to the commissioners. He assumed that he would predecease those aspects of the treaty that were due to lapse in twenty years. The only issue Charles continued to stick over was the episcopal estates, protesting that he could not alienate what he did not own.

The demands, as draconian as they were, did not please many in the army, who trusted neither king nor Parliament. When an agreement was nearly secured by 5 December 1648, the sudden intervention of the army finished all further talk of treaties. The soldiers marched to Westminster and forcibly purged those members of the Commons who had favoured a settlement with the king. Some were arrested and imprisoned, some detained and the largest number simply sent home.

Pride's Purge ended the Treaty of Newport and prevented the king from accepting the Presbyterian terms of settlement. The remaining members of the House of Commons, under the watchful eye of the army, now proceeded with the soldiers' demand that the king be brought to trial and held accountable for nearly a decade of misery. Royalists had anticipated nearly every possible outcome but this: the public trial of the monarch. After years of pleading with

Charles to accept any terms that would restore his throne, they now worried that he was conceding too much. Unlike subsequent generations of critics, they believed that if he gave his word, he would stick to it. The army was equally fearful, believing that Charles would somehow escape culpability. It determined on a trial though it appeared that no consensus yet existed on the question of punishment.

Once again Charles was removed from the care of parliamentary commissioners and into the hands of the soldiers. He was taken in stages back to Windsor Castle under close guard and none too courteous care. There he was deprived of both companionship and correspondence, except what could be ingeniously smuggled in to him. Though he had access to his library and his garden, he appeared to be an isolated figure with a room in a tower. Charles served as his own chaplain and led his remaining personal servants through the Christmas festivities. His captivity, cruel treatment and sense of injured innocence made for predictable comparisons to the life of Christ. It is not at all clear how much he knew of the preparations being made at Westminster, where MPs and lawyers worked to create laws under which he could be tried and to empanel a court to do the work. But he knew enough to declare that he would not recognize the legality of a newly created court. Rumours of last-minute schemes to have him accept harsher terms or even abdicate in favour of his youngest son swirled around London; they were reported to the Royalists in France, who also continued to dream of last-minute foreign intervention. But as the New Year turned, the more knowing agents sensed an insatiable desire for revenge radiating from the army.

The trial began on 12 January but the king was not summoned until the 20th. Its presiding officer was John Bradshaw, Chief Justice of Chester, and the only sitting judge willing to accept the task. Charles wore a black cloak embroidered with a large silver Garter star and a stovepipe hat in place of a crown. He sat in a red velvet chair behind the bar from where the prosecutor and the judge harangued him. When he first entered the courtroom, he was menaced by the troops ostensibly present to protect him, and when the silver head of his cane fell to the ground, no one bent to retrieve it. Symbolic or not, all of this was in marked contrast to his treatment just weeks before and must have impressed upon him the seriousness of his situation. His refusal to recognize the court or to plead to its charges was his only legal alternative and had the added benefit of infuriating Justice Bradshaw, who incompetently conducted the proceedings. Charles could hardly deny that he had been present on the battlefields specified in the indictment and, therefore, had made war against Parliament. This was the newly legislated standard for treason; a charge once designed to protect kings but now refashioned to menace one. Nor was he likely to win a point by arguing that such actions were not crimes when they had been committed. Three times he was brought before the court and three times he showed them the regal face of a monarch. He questioned the underlying legitimacy of the court and the legality of the process. For a moment it looked as if his logic might disrupt the proceedings. But the decision had been made to press forward whatever the cost and the king's refusal to plead was, by the practice of the day, taken as an admission of guilt. As the sentence was passed, Charles lost his composure for the only time. He called out that he wished to meet with Parliament to present them with proposals for the good of the kingdom. His pleas went unheard. A mock trial preceded a real execution.

Charles's last days were calmly spent. He bowed to the inevitable and prepared for the eternal. He wrote a brief political testament for his son, urging him to defend the established Church, to rule justly and to forgo revenge for the good of his people. He conducted a tearful and touching interview with his youngest children and instructed Prince Henry to resist the blandishments of his captors should they attempt to place him on the throne. He was finally allowed some religious solace when Bishop Juxon was admitted to pray with him. He distributed his few remaining personal effects, a watch fob, an elaborately bound prayer book and, to Colonel Matthew Tomlinson, who had shown him kindness during his final imprisonment, a golden toothpick. His appearance on the scaffold in a white satin cap and two shirts, which he wore so that he wouldn't shiver and seem afraid, made a deep impression upon observers. He remained composed until he saw the metal staples that had been driven into the platform to restrain him if it proved necessary. He had never thought of such an unseemly act of desperation. His words could hardly be heard amid the hum of the crowd and the howl of the wind: 'I go from a corruptible to an incorruptible crown; where no disturbance can be, no disturbance in the world.'[5] His more powerful thoughts were already circulating in London. The *Eikon Basilike*, which comprised his own explanations and justifications for his actions during the war, supplemented by prayers composed by the clergyman John Gauden, became an international sensation. 'I am the martyr of the people,' he said on the scaffold, and the *Eikon* was his testament.[6] The Christ-like imagery would prove deeply effective propaganda: transforming defeat into victorious sacrifice, and holding out hope that the House of Stuart might one day experience a resurrection.

At 2 o'clock on Monday 30 January 1649, the executioner's axe fell true and the head of Charles Stuart, King of Scotland, Ireland and England, was severed from his body. Charles made a good end according to seventeenth-century conventions. He forgave his oppressors, prayed for his own salvation and passed into history.

Notes

Contemporary tracts are cited with their bibliographical identification numbers. A number preceded by no letter is from A. W. Pollard and G. R. Redgrave (eds), *A Short-Title Catalogue of Books Printed in England, Scotland and Ireland, and of English Books Printed Abroad, 1475–1640*, 2nd edn, 2 vols (London: 1988 and 1991). A capital letter followed by a number is from Donald Wing, *Short-Title Catalogue of Books Printed in England, Scotland, Ireland, Wales, and British North America and of English Books Printed in Other Countries 1640–1700*, 2nd edn, 3 vols (New York: 1994). The letter 'E.' (with a full point) followed by a number is from G. K. Fortescue (ed.), *Catalogue of the Pamphlets, Books, Newspapers, and Manuscripts ... Collected by George Thomason, 1640–1661*, 2 vols (London: 1908).

PROLOGUE

1. S5053. Thomas Sprat, *A Sermon Preached before the Honourable House of Commons* (London: 1678), p. 21.
2. L2228. William Lilly, *Monarchy or No Monarchy* (London: 1651), p. 79.
3. Peter Heylyn, *Observations on the History of the Reign of Charles I* (London: 1656), pp. 105–6.
4. Sir Philip Warwick, *Memoirs of the Reign of King Charles I* (Edinburgh: J. Ballantyne, 1813), p. 9.
5. E2221D. *A Remonstrance of the State of the Kingdom* (London: 1641), p. 4.
6. J. P. Kenyon, *The Stuarts* (London: B. T. Batsford, 1958), p. 64.
7. Charles Carlton, *Charles I: The Personal Monarch*, 2nd edn (London: Routledge, 1995), p. xiii.
8. Maurice Lee, Jnr, *The Road to Revolution: Scotland under Charles I, 1625–37* (Urbana: University of Illinois Press, 1985), p. 5.
9. Peter Donald, *An Uncounselled King: Charles I and the Scottish Troubles, 1637–1641* (Cambridge: Cambridge University Press, 1990), p. 14.
10. L. J. Reeve, *Charles I and the Road to Personal Rule* (Cambridge: Cambridge University Press, 1989), p. 173.
11. Conrad Russell, *The Causes of the English Civil War* (Oxford: Oxford University Press, 1990), p. 206.
12. G. M. Trevelyan, *England Under the Stuarts* (London: Methuen, 1949), p. 179.
13. Austin Woolrych, *Britain in Revolution 1625–1660* (Oxford: Oxford University Press, 2002), p. 50.

14. Keith Brown, 'Aristocratic Finances and the Origins of the Scottish Revolution', *English Historical Review*, 104 (1989), p. 84.
15. Christopher Hill, *The Century of Revolution* (New York: W. W. Norton, 1961), p. 74.
16. Woolrych, *Britain in Revolution*, p. 51.
17. Warwick, *Memoirs of the Reign of King Charles I*, p. 334.
18. William Knowler, *The Earl of Strafforde's Letters and Dispatches*, 2 vols (London: 1739), vol. 2, p. 32.
19. Edward Hyde, Earl of Clarendon, *The Life of the Earl of Clarendon*, 2 vols (Oxford: Oxford University Press, 1857), vol. 1, pp. 136–7.
20. Richard Cust, *Charles I: A Political Life* (Harlow: Longman, 2005), p. 240.
21. Thomas Babington Macaulay, *Critical, Historical, and Miscellaneous Essays and Poems*, 3 vols (Chicago: Donohue & Henneberry, 1885), vol. 3, p. 375.
22. Russell, *Causes of the English Civil War*, p. 194.
23. L2228. Lilly, *Monarchy or No Monarchy*, p. 119.
24. H171. John Hacket, *Scrinia Reserata* (London: 1693), part 2, p. 162.

I. PRINCE AND KING

1. L2228. Lilly, *Monarchy or No Monarchy*, p. 82.
2. Sir Robert Carey, *Memoirs of Sir Robert Carey* (Edinburgh: Constable, 1808), p. 138.
3. M. Jansson and W. Bidwell (eds), *Proceedings in Parliament 1625* (New Haven, Conn.: Yale University Press, 1987), p. 29. Charles quotes from Acts 22:3, where the verse continues 'and taught according to the perfect manner of the law of the fathers'.
4. L2228. Lilly, *Monarchy or No Monarchy*, p. 76.
5. Nicholas Cranfield, 'George Carleton (1557/8–1628)', in *Oxford Dictionary of Biography* (Oxford: Oxford University Press, 2004).
6. M. A. E. Green, *Elizabeth, Electress Palatine and Queen of Bohemia*, ed. S. C. Lomas (London: Methuen, 1909), p. 24.
7. 14344. *The Workes of the Most High and Mightie Prince, James* (London: 1616), title page.
8. James Spedding et al. (eds), *The Collected Works of Francis Bacon*, 15 vols (London: Longman, 1857–74), vol. 13, p. 55.
9. Shakespeare, *Hamlet* I.ii.11.
10. Brennan Pursell, *The Winter King* (Aldershot: Ashgate, 2003), p. 17.
11. A. B. Hinds (ed.), *Calendar of State Papers and Manuscripts Relating to English Affairs Existing in the Collections and Archives of Venice, and in Other Libraries of Northern Italy, 1619–1621* (London: 1910), p. 433.
12. C186. *Cabala: Mysteries of State and Government* (London: 1691), p. 330.

2. WARS AND PARLIAMENTS

1. C2535. *The papers which passed at New-Castle betwixt His Sacred Majestie and Mr Alex. Henderson: concerning the change of church-government. Anno Dom. 1646* (London: 1649), p. 2.

2. John Bruce (ed.), *Calendar of State Papers, Domestic Series, Charles I*, 23 vols (London: 1858–97), *Addenda 1625–49*, p. 1.

3. H171. Hacket, *Scrinia Reserata*, vol. 2, pp. 2, 4.

4. *Historical Manuscripts Commission, Eleventh Report, Appendix, Part 1*, p. 22 (Salvetti, 17/27 June 1625); C186. *Cabala*, p. 302.

5. Sir Henry Ellis, *Original Letters*, 1st Series, 3 vols (London: 1824), vol. 3, p. 198.

6. Pauline Gregg, *King Charles I* (Berkeley, Calif.: University of California Press, 1981), p. 97.

7. M. Jansson and W. Bidwell (eds), *Proceedings in Parliament, 1625* (New Haven, Conn.: Yale University Press, 1987), p. 276.

8. Ibid., p. 133.

9. Ellis, *Original Letters*, 1st Series, vol. 3, p. 206.

10. Mary Everett Green (ed.), *Letters of Queen Henrietta Maria* (London: R. Bentley, 1857), p. 4.

11. Isaac D'Israeli, *Commentaries on the Life and Reign of Charles I, King of England* (Paris: A. and W. Galignani, 1851), p. 62.

12. J. O. Halliwell, *Letters of the Kings of England*, 2 vols (London: H. Colburn, 1846), vol. 2, p. 270.

13. M. Jansson and W. Bidwell (eds), *Proceedings in Parliament, 1626*, 3 vols (New Haven, Conn.: Yale University Press, 1991), vol. 2, p. 249.

14. Ibid., p. 284.

15. Ibid., p. 282.

16. Ibid., p. 391.

17. Philip Yorke (ed.), *Miscellaneous State Papers from 1501–1726*, 2 vols (London: 1778), vol. 2, p. 20.

18. R. C. Johnson, M. F. Keeler et al. (eds), *Commons Debates, 1628*, 4 vols (New Haven, Conn.: Yale University Press, 1977–83), vol. 2, p. 58.

19. Ibid., p. 203.

20. Ibid., p. 309.

21. Johnson, Keeler et al. (eds), *Commons Debates, 1628*, vol. 4, p. 352.

22. J. F. Larkin (ed.), *Stuart Royal Proclamations: Royal Proclamations of Charles I*, 2 vols (Oxford: Clarendon Press, 1973 and 1983), vol. 2, pp. 227–8.

3. PEACE AND PROSPERITY

1. David L. Smith, 'The Fourth Earl of Dorset and the Personal Rule of Charles I', *Journal of British Studies*, 30 (1991), p. 277.

2. Green (ed.), *Letters of Queen Henrietta Maria*, pp. 15–16.

3. Gregg, *King Charles I*, p. 189.

4. Alison Plowden, *Henrietta Maria* (Stroud: Sutton, 2001), p. 97.

5. 4620. Thomas Carew, *Poems* (London: 1640), p. 96; W. D. Macray (ed.), *Clarendon's History of the Rebellion and Civil Wars in England*, 6 vols (Oxford: Clarendon Press, 1888), vol. 1, p. 93.

6. J. Franklin Jameson (ed.), *Johnson's Wonder-Working Providence 1628–1651* (New York: C. Scribner's Sons, 1910), p. 23.

7. William Scott and James Bliss (eds), *The Works of William Laud*, 7 vols (Oxford: John Henry Parker, 1847–60), vol. 6, part 1, p. 293.

8. Psalm 96:9.

4. IRELAND AND SCOTLAND

1. Knowler, *Strafforde's Letters and Dispatches*, vol. 2, p. 187.

2. 21906a. Walter Balcanquhall, in *A Large Declaration Concerning the Late Tumults in Scotland* (London: 1639), p. 18.

3. Anthony Milton, 'Laud, William (1573–1645)', in *Oxford Dictionary of National Biography* (Oxford: Oxford University Press, 2004).

4. David Laing (ed.), *The Letters and Journals of Robert Baillie*, 3 vols (Edinburgh: Bannatyne Club, 1841–2), vol. 1, p. 541.

5. Ibid., p. 86.

6. Gilbert Burnet, *The Memoires of the Lives and Actions of James and William, Dukes of Hamilton and Castleherald* (London: 1677), p. 43.

7. 21906a. Balcanquhall, in *Large Declaration*, p. 86.

8. Burnet, *Lives of the Dukes of Hamilton*, p. 60.

9. S. R. Gardiner (ed.), *The Hamilton Papers*, Camden Society, New Series, 27 (London: 1880), p. 3.

10. Burnet, *Lives of the Dukes of Hamilton*, p. 55.

11. Gardiner, *Hamilton Papers*, p. 55.

12. Larkin (ed.), *Stuart Royal Proclamations*, vol. 2, p. 665.

13. 21906a. Balcanquhall, in *Large Declaration*, p. 5.

14. Richard Scrope and Thomas Monkhouse (eds), *State Papers Collected by Edward, Earl of Clarendon*, 3 vols (Oxford: 1767–86), vol. 2, p. 81.

5. REFORM AND REBELLION

1. Laing (ed.), *Letters of Robert Baillie*, vol. 1, p. 309.

2. Knowler, *Strafforde's Letters and Dispatches*, vol. 2, p. 416.

3. *Journals of the House of Lords*, 123 vols (London: 1509–1891), vol. 4, p. 310.

4. John Foster, *The Debates on the Grand Remonstrance* (London: John Murray, 1860), p. 292.

5. John Rushworth, *Historical Collections*, 8 vols (London: 1721–2), vol. 3, pp. 532–3.

6. Ibid.

7. Burnet, *Lives of the Dukes of Hamilton*, p. 203.

8. Hyde, *Life of the Earl of Clarendon*, vol. 1, p. 178.
9. E.292 (27). *The King's Cabinet Opened: Or, certain packets of secret letters & papers* (London: 1645), p. 7.

6. REVOLUTION AND REGICIDE

1. Laing, *Letters of Robert Baillie*, vol. 2, p. 362.
2. M2161A. John Milton, 'On the New Forcers of Conscience Under the Long Parliament', *Poems, &c. Upon Several Occasions* (London: 1673), p. 69.
3. John Bruce, *Charles I in 1646*, Camden Society, Old Series, 63 (London: 1856), p. 45.
4. Warwick, *Memoirs of the Reign of King Charles I*, pp. 336–7.
5. C2792bA. *King Charles His Speech Made upon the Scaffold at Whitehall-Gate* (London: 1649), p. 8.
6. Ibid., p. 6.

Further Reading

There are a host of biographies of Charles I, of which Richard Cust, *Charles I: A Political Life* (Harlow: Longman, 2005), is the most balanced and Charles Carlton, *Charles I: The Personal Monarch*, 2nd edn (London: Routledge, 1995), the most opinionated. The essays in Thomas Corns (ed.), *The Royal Image: Representations of Charles I* (Cambridge: Cambridge University Press, 1999), offer insights into the rich artistic culture of the era. General surveys of the period abound, though none take the purview of the entire reign. For sheer pleasure, the outstanding narrative is by C. V. Wedgewood, which extends over three volumes: *The King's Peace, 1637–1641* (London: Collins, 1955); *The King's War, 1641–1647* (London: Collins, 1958); *The Trial of Charles I* (Harmondsworth: Penguin, 1963). Conrad Russell, *Parliaments and English Politics, 1621–1629* (Oxford: Oxford University Press, 1979), offers unique insight into the relations between Charles and his early assemblies. Kevin Sharpe, *The Personal Rule of Charles I* (New Haven, Conn., and London: Yale University Press, 1993), is a doorstop of a book but conveys a fresh perspective on the 1630s. The religious history of the reign is best entered through Nicholas Tyacke, *Anti-Calvinists* (Oxford: Oxford University Press, 1987). David Stevenson, *The Scottish Revolution 1637–1644* (Newton Abbot: David & Charles, 1973), holds up well as an account of Scottish politics, while Aidan Clarke, *The Old English in Ireland* (London: MacGibbon & Kee, 1966), remains indispensable. To sample the confidence of an earlier generation, nothing is more infuriating than Lawrence Stone, *The Causes of the English Revolution* (New York: Harper & Row, 1965). John Morrill best represents the local perspective on the war in *Revolt in the Provinces* (London: Longman, 1996);

while the outstanding recent survey is Michael Braddick, *God's Fury, England's Fire* (London: Penguin, 2008). David Underdown, *Pride's Purge* (Oxford: Clarendon Press, 1971), is a landmark of modern scholarship on the revolution that replaced the king.

Sources for study of the reign of Charles I are beyond abundant. Barry Coward and Peter Gaunt (eds), *English Historical Documents 1603–1660* (London: Routledge, 2010), contains excerpts from hundreds of primary documents. There is no modern edition of the king's writings, but a selection is presented in Charles Petrie (ed.), *Letters, Speeches and Proclamations of Charles I* (London: Cassell, 1935). All of Charles's proclamations have been edited by J. F. Larkin (ed.), *Stuart Royal Proclamations: Proclamations of Charles I, 1625–1646* (Oxford: Oxford University Press, 1983). The great contemporary account of the reign is W. D. Macray (ed.), *The History of the Rebellion and Civil Wars in England by Edward, Earl of Clarendon*, 6 vols (Oxford: Clarendon Press, 1888). David Lagomarsino and Charles Wood, *The Trial of Charles I* (Hanover, NH: Dartmouth College Press, 1989), contains contemporary accounts of the king's trial, while Jim Daems and Holly Nelson (eds), *Eikon Basilike* (Peterborough, Ontario: Broadview Editions, 2006), is a modern edition of one of the most influential works of the seventeenth century.

Picture Credits

1. Charles, Duke of York, 1613, by Robert Peake the Elder (© The Old Schools, University of Cambridge)
2. King Charles I and Henrietta Maria, 1632, by Gonzales Coques (possibly) after Van Dyck (© Victoria and Albert Museum, London)
3. Charles I and Henrietta Maria with Prince Charles and Princess Mary (detail), 1632, by Sir Anthony van Dyck. (Royal Collection Trust © Her Majesty Queen Elizabeth II, 2014/Bridgeman Images)
4. Charles I with M. de St Antoine, 1633, by Sir Anthony van Dyck (The Royal Collection Trust © Her Majesty Queen Elizabeth II, 2014/Bridgeman Images
5. Charles I in three positions, 1635, by Sir Anthony van Dyck (The Royal Collection Trust © Her Majesty Queen Elizabeth II, 2014/Bridgeman Images)
6. William Laud (detail), c.1635–7, by Sir Anthony van Dyck (© Fitzwilliam Museum, University of Cambridge, UK/Bridgeman Images)
7. Thomas Wentworth, 1st Earl of Strafford, c.1633-6, by Sir Anthony van Dyck (Private Collection/Bridgeman Images)
8. Charles I, c.1637–8, by Sir Anthony van Dyck (National Gallery, London, UK/Bridgeman Images)
9. Charles I at his trial, 1648, by Edward Bower (Antony House, Cornwall/National Trust Photographic Library/John Hammond/Bridgeman Images)

Acknowledgements

In writing this book, I have incurred many debts. Simon Winder took a chance by assigning me a task in which I have previously been defeated and made a number of valuable suggestions to improve the text. I hope his confidence has been rewarded. If no man is a hero to his butler, no author escapes the withering eye of his copy-editor. Kate Parker translated this text into British English and saved me from infelicities great and small. Several friends have read drafts of the text and offered criticisms and corrections. I would like to thank Mike Braddick, Tom Cogswell, Jeff Collins, Maya Jasanoff, Molly McClain, John Morrill, Eric Nelson, Barbara Shapiro, Scott Sowerby and Max Straus for finding the errors that escaped my jaundiced eye. If I have imparted meaning to the life of Charles I, the dedicatees have done the same for me.

Index